FANGED: BLOOD AND WATER

FANGED: BLOOD AND WATER

TIANNA LE'RAY

NEW DEGREE PRESS

COPYRIGHT © 2021 TIANNA LE'RAY

FANGED: BLOOD AND WATER

ISBN   978-1-63730-449-5   *Paperback*
        978-1-63730-555-3   *Kindle Ebook*
        978-1-63730-556-0   *Ebook*

DEDICATION

To my Biggest Supporters!

First, thank you to Brittni Smith! If it weren't for you, I would never have gotten into writing. You were my true inspiration as a kid, and I would never have fallen in love with my passion if you hadn't showed me what it looked like. I love you, sis!

Next thanks goes to Miguel Garcia, I know I must have driven you crazy with all my phone calls and long, long conversations about my book. If it weren't for you, this book would not be the finalized concept that it is. So, thank you for cheering me on and listening to all my crazy ideas.

Lastly thank you to my mother, Cheryl Clarke. You never stopped cheering me on and never put me down. You always made me feel like my story was worth sharing. You listened to every crazy story idea and helped me problem-solve. You never complained hearing my story through its first to fifth edit. This story would not exist without your love and support. I love you, mom!

This book would never have been a reality if it weren't for you all.

IN LOVING MEMORY OF

Maureen Roach and Simeon Bradshaw, thank you for your
loving support and I know you all are watching over me.

CONTENTS

CHAPTER 1

SILAS

Monsters are real.

Monsters are raw, cruel, and vicious. Sure humans can be evil, but the monsters I know made serial killer's work look like child's play. They creep through the night, devouring their victims whole. They are powerful. Hell, some are even invincible. They live among us, they are your teachers, your neighbors, your friends. You wouldn't know they weren't human until it was too late. Most monsters wear a mask. A human face but with something dark and sinister lurking underneath. I should know, I was one of them. Well, half of one anyway. You don't have to believe me, hell I didn't believe it either until I saw my mother kill a man for the first time.

I was constantly at war. Be it with other monsters or myself. Monsters of all kinds have tried to kill me, but none succeeded. All that is thanks to Mommy Dearest. See my mother didn't like anyone touching what was hers and for the longest time, that's what I was. Hers. That is until I turned eighteen. I left in the daylight when Mother or her minions couldn't stop me. I never turned back, never stopped running.

It had been ten long years since I last saw my family and I planned to keep it that way.

That's when I found myself in New York, the Big Apple itself. Enjoying the bustling streets and heavy traffic. The city has always been a place I called home. Didn't matter where, the hustle and bustle was in my blood. The only thing I hated about cities was the beggars. Some were just poor while others were cons well placed and set on sucking the pockets of passersby dry. And some of them were just bounty hunters hunting their next prey.

I sat down on the hard pavement, my ass numb from the October wind. A woman wearing a long black dress walked by and dropped a quarter into my jar. I whispered my thanks as she gingerly walked away on her four-inch high heels. I leaned my head back against the wall, wiping away my jet-black hair from my eyes. I glanced around taking in my surroundings. I had made camp near an outdated electronics repair shop. Across the street were other businesses: a cheap Chinese takeout joint, a chiropractor, and a pawn shop. The streets were nearly empty save for the few night owls going to the bar.

My bounty was simple. A monster was picking off the homeless like a hand in a bowl of chips. He was a low level. Worth no more than a grand. Sure, I could have gone after a big bounty, but I wanted an easy night. I was still sore from my last encounter two nights prior with a ghoul that was terrorizing a college campus. Catching my prey was easy. All I had to do was set out the right bait.

I took out a small knife from my pocket and unfolded it, revealing a sharp blade. I ran the knife against my thumb and let my blood drip to the ground. My blood was a rare treat. You see there aren't too many Dhampirs or human vampire hybrids in the world and, from what I've heard, our blood is exquisite. It was only a matter of time before my bounty smelt it and tracked me down. I let my hand bleed for about three minutes before I wiped my finger onto my pants. Now was the hard part: the waiting game.

Taking on monsters is no easy feat. Most monsters are stronger, faster, and have more endurance than your average human. Some have lived for many years and over that time gained a large array of knowledge. Though I wasn't fully human and was blessed with some abilities, I was still pretty weak in the monster realm. I was a whopping six feet tall, thin with, dare I say, only a little muscle definition. To most monsters I was a chew toy. I turned my attention to my wristwatch and that's when I heard it, the monster approaching. Wow, five minutes, a new record.

Its entrance wasn't subtle. The monster was practically running down the middle of the street, claws clicking loudly against the asphalt. An American Werewolf. The perfect fusion between man and wolf. The werewolf ran on all fours, appearing at about four feet tall. It bore a long muzzle and piercing yellow eyes that glowed in the night. Its skin was a slate gray with hints of blue. A long ridge of hair ran down its back all the way to its short nub of a tail. Seeing as it made no move to conceal itself, I rationalized that the werewolf was a newborn, freshly turned. It must have given into its blood lust and ran rampant. I waited until it was nearly upon me before pulling out my 9mm.

I performed a tuck and roll, avoiding the massive beast. The werewolf went at full speed and charged into the electronic repair shop. It crashed against the window display, shards of glass running down its head and neck. The scent of metallic sting wafted through the air. Werewolf blood, unlike Dhampir blood, was *not* exquisite. My nose curled up, trying to push away the smell that I could only equate to rotten eggs. I rose from the ground, aiming my 9mm at the creature's head. A large paw swiped at my hand and knocked my gun away into the open road.

Damn, it was fast. The creature rose to its full height, towering above me. It was an overpowering seven feet tall. The creature pounced on me, claws slicing open my shoulder. I gritted my teeth as the ground came up to meet us. I held on to the beast's head as its jaws worked furiously, trying to bite its way into my chest. Stringy spit landed on my shirt and my stomach wrenched in disgust. I released my left hand from under its jaw and reached into my pocket to pull out my knife. One-handed, I opened the knife and jammed it into the creature's eye. Its head rocked back, a howl of pain roaring through the air.

I scooted out from underneath him, pushing myself onto my feet. With the creature distracted I picked up my 9mm and checked that it still was functional. The beast crashed into me. I went flying and crashed down on the other side of the street. I sat up, trying to bring air into my lungs. Damn bastard took me out when I was distracted. A noise that could only be described as a course laugh filled the air. It was laughing at me—the damn werewolf was laughing at me. I sat up, anger flaring. I got to my feet, my side groaning with pain. Somehow through the brunt force of the attack, I had managed to hold on to my gun. I cocked it and fired a shot at the beast's back knee. It hit with a sickening crunch. The beast yowled, skittering off balance.

I released a single laugh. "Ain't so funny now huh Fuzzy?"

Fuzzy growled and charged once more, running only on three legs. It was slower this time. I stood rooted to the spot, took aim, and fired. The bullet whizzed through the air before landing square in the beast's chest. It crashed to the ground, panting heavily. I took a knee, pulling out a large silver dagger strapped to my calf. I walked over to the beast, towering over its crumpled form. The werewolf was at the end of the line. Its body began to contort and spasm. In seconds a naked human male lay before me. His curling brown hair covered his golden eyes. His body was thin, emaciated, and pale. He was no older than fifteen. He was a child, no wonder he couldn't control the blood lust.

He raised his hand weakly in the air. "Please, don't kill me."

His words were rough and cut through me like a knife. I stood there unable to move. How could I kill a child? He was by no means innocent, but he hadn't chosen this. To be a monster. I reminded myself I was doing him a service. Killing him meant people stayed safe. Killing him meant that he would never have to fight that blood lust ever again. Killing him meant … that I would be giving in to my monster's wishes. The silver knife clacked to the ground. I couldn't do it. Every inch of me screamed *kill the monster*, but that meant losing my humanity.

That was just something I just couldn't afford to lose. After growing up and seeing the carnage and damage my mother had caused, I vowed to keep my humanity. It was something I would protect with every fiber of my being. Keeping my humanity meant that I was better than them, that I wouldn't stoop to a monster's twisted way of being. It means I was never going to let in my dark side. I pulled out my cell phone, punching in a single number on speed dial. The phone rang two times before a deep voice answered.

"Yes."

"I have caught the bounty number 3568923," I said into the phone.

"What is the status?"

"Alive, but subdued."

"Your location?"

"South Lenox Street."

"We will send out the cleaners your way. Stay put."

The man hung up, leaving me in the streets with a monster now turned boy. I made my way over to my corner and grabbed the blanket that had been wrapped around me minutes before. I walked over to the monster, draping the blanket over his body. I sat down beside him, Glock resting in my lap. The boy shivered away, only managing to move about an inch. His golden eyes stared up at me.

"You really aren't going to kill me?" His voice came out barely a whisper.

I sighed, hitting the gun lightly against my temple. "You'll be sent to Rehab. You'll be transferred to Sable, Pennsylvania."

"Why Pennsylvania?" He asked, suppressing a shiver.

"New York's is full and they want you away from your Alpha. Now if you don't fuck it up, they'll let you leave alive and hopefully, you'll be able to live a life as close to normal as possible. If you do fuck it up, they send me."

It took about five minutes before the cleaning crew arrived in big white vans. They hustled out of their vehicles like a miniature army. Two men knelt down beside the boy, placing him on a stretcher. The boy, out of pain, began to refuse so I cocked my gun in response. The boy went quiet; guess Fuzzy was a good boy after all. I smiled lightly and holstered my gun underneath my jacket. The boy was loaded into the Cleaner's van and, just as quickly as they had come, they vanished. I was left alone standing in the street.

I looked around assessing the damage, something I would have to report. There wasn't much, surprisingly, just the broken window of the electronic repair shop. Something that would probably be blamed as an attempted break-in or young hooligans having fun with rocks.

The cold wind cut through my skin. I looked down at my torn and dirty shirt. Damn, I needed a drink. I went back to my corner collecting my begging jar. I shook the change into my hand. A whopping seventy-five cents. Sighing, I tossed the jar in a nearby trash can. After a night like this, I was heading to On the Rocks.

***

On the Rocks was a local dive bar, home to all the nitty-gritty nasties in the Big Apple. I pushed past the swinging door and was immediately assaulted with the smell of cigarette smoke. Smoking was abolished indoors in bars in the nineties, but here no one cared. I resisted the urge to wave my hand in front of my face.

On the Rocks was your typical bar, eight tables lined up in pairs were spread out all along the floor. A pool table, currently occupied by burly men, sat in the corner across from the dartboard. A bar sat to the far side, lit up like the fourth of July with bright lights, alcohol, and shiny glasses. Photographs of New York's key attractions coated the walls. I looked at a piece of the Statue of Liberty, it had a strange brown tint. Funny—I remembered the picture being green the last time I saw it. I walked up to the bar, then set my hands at rest on the counter.

"Hey Phil," I said.

"Silas. How's it been, man?" he asked, preparing a gin and tonic. He worked with such precision and speed, one could call it art. I watched him as he mixed the drink, eyes landing on the skin of his forearm hidden by a long sleeve. As he moved, his shirt sleeve revealed small green scales. Phil, as I had learned from my many visits, was part Nix: a sea monster that often bred with humans.

"Hellish," I said, grabbing my sleeve twice. Phil looked down, eyes growing slightly wider, and adjusted his own. He nodded his thanks. We half-humans had to look out for one another.

"Tell me about it."

"Work is kicking my ass."

"Ain't it for everyone?" He passed the gin and tonic to a blonde. "What are you having?"

"Jack and Coke."

Phil nodded, hands moving at light speed. He had the drink in front of me in seconds. "So what's really bugging you?"

"It was a kid. Couldn't have been older than fifteen. Turned and gave into blood lust. I couldn't …" I felt the icy glass against my fingertips and took a sip. "I should've done it, you know? Saved humanity and all that shit."

"You did save humanity, Silas. Your own. Remember you're only half-human so you have to work twice as hard. Humanity isn't something we were born with, it's something we fight for every day. Take my family for example, they love the water. I do too, but they also enjoy drowning helpless victims. And as much as I want to say that's a horrible thing, there is something in my DNA that tells me do it. I have to resist, no matter how strong the pull, because I want to be human. Whether it's a big battle or small, choosing to be human is always right. Get me, man?"

"Damn Phil. Getting all soft on me."

Phil grabbed a dishrag and began shining a wine glass. I nodded at Phil, his words of wisdom washing over me. I turned and walked away from the bar. I made my way past a crowd of young bloods and parked my ass in the corner with the dartboard. The blonde with the gin and tonic approached, hips swaying to the dull roar of the music. Maple, as I'd come to know her, ran this bar like it was the streets. Finding innocent and dumb victims to sleep with. She casually took a seat on my lap, brushing a strand of hair from her eyes.

"Hey, Suga," she whispered, planting a kiss on my cheek. I welcomed it; I mean what man wouldn't? I ran my hand through her hair and sipped on my Jack and Coke. I forced myself to smile, but I just wasn't feeling it. She wiggled her ass in my lap playfully. "So Suga, you busy tonight?"

I thought about it for a moment. I could take her up on her offer and welcome myself into the world of STDs or I could politely decline. After all, tonight was a rough night. I stood up swiftly. The woman's heels clicked onto the floor but she couldn't keep her balance. I excused myself, walking away and downing my whole drink.

***

I was about seven drinks in and wasn't ready to quit, but Phil cut me off. I sat slumped in the corner barely able to stay conscious. The blonde had moved on to another victim, a young frat boy. Something was buzzing against my leg. I shook away the feeling and tried to keep from leaning my head against the wall, but the buzzing didn't stop. I reached down into my pocket, pulling out my phone. It buzzed once more. I looked at the screen and was met with an unknown number.

Against my better judgment, I slid my thumb on the screen to answer the call.

"Hello," I whispered into the phone, slurring. "You better not be a telemarketer."

"Hello, Son," a voice whispered back.

My head cleared instantly. I bit back the bile rising in my throat. I couldn't speak, couldn't think. My heart pounded in my chest and my breath was caught in my lungs.

"It's been a long time."

I sat still, unmoving. *How had she found my number? Has she found my location? Where was she now?* That's when I felt it, the panic. I had to get out of there. To run far away and never stop running.

The voice on the phone dragged me out of my thoughts. "My sweet beloved Silas. Don't you think it's time to come home?"

And with that, the line was disconnected. I wobbled up onto my feet, forced myself to draw in a breath, and made my way to the back door. I exited the bar, numb, not even sure where I was headed. *Was home safe? Would she be waiting for me there?* I shook my head sharply, shaking away the thoughts. I needed to keep my wits about me. Screwing up would cost me a price I didn't want to pay. First things first, I needed to get my things, then disconnect my phone, and lastly leave that godforsaken city.

CHAPTER 2

HARPER

College Algebra wasn't my thing.

I had spent the whole day studying. I know it's a little obsessive to study for an entire day but I wanted to keep up my straight A streak. I leaned back in my seat, stretching. Alice, a friend I made when I first started attending college, sat across the table. She ran a pale hand through her blonde hair. She then slammed her face against the wooden table, groaning.

"I don't think I can study anymore," she said, "my brain seriously hurts."

I sighed, feeling a similar pressure in the middle of my brain. I massaged my temples. "Alice, you got this. Just two more hours and I'm sure we will get this down perfectly."

"I'm not like you Harper. You are smart. I mean you made Dean's List as long as I've known you."

"You can make Dean's List too," I said.

"C's get degrees. I need coffee. You want?"

"I'll get it."

I got up from my seat and left the study room. I walked about fifteen feet until I ran into the Espresso Bean, our campus' best coffee shop. It was nothing compared to Starbucks, but once you've stayed up all night studying you could barely tell the difference. Shoot, most things in North Haven, Washington were sucky but, again, once you got used to it you could barely tell the difference.

I waited my turn in line and ordered upon reaching the counter. An iced chai for me and two shots of straight espresso for Alice. Once finished I took the collection of drinks back to the study room, lightly sipping on my chai. I handed Alice her espresso and she greedily took it with a whispered thanks. She downed the bitter espresso and continued to rest her head on the table, long blonde hair fanning out.

It was times like these where I wanted to be real with Alice. She had become a close friend. She and Dru were the only two I could trust. I wanted to look into her bright blue eyes and tell her everything. I took a seat at the table with a sigh.

"What's bothering you?" Alice asked, not lifting her head.

"It's nothing, just getting a headache."

I leaned my head forward, curls falling across my face. I sat like that for some time, eventually dozing off. Then I felt a buzzing in my pocket. I lifted my weary head up and pulled out my cell from my pants pocket. I glanced at the screen: Dru's name blinking in white. Smiling, I brought the phone to my ear.

"Hello love," I said.

"Harper. Oh thank god."

"Dru, is everything ok?" I asked, standing up.

Alice lifted her head up looking at me, a worried look on her face. Panic began running rampantly through my body. My palms got sweaty, and I nearly dropped my phone.

I quickly began collecting my things and shoving them into my backpack. I holstered it onto my shoulder, walked to the door, and entered the hall. "Dru? Can you hear me?"

A student from a neighboring study room peeked his head from behind a cracked door and shushed me. I whispered a quick apology as the student slammed the door shut.

"Harper, everything okay?" Alice asked, coming out the room.

"Don't come home," Dru said on the line.

"Why? What's wrong?"

"The house ..."

The phone line clicked off and I stood still, unable to think. Something was wrong. I shook my head in disbelief. Someone must have found out about me. Then dread hit my heart. Was Dru okay? She said not to come home.

"Harper ..."

"I'm sorry Alice but I need to go," I said quickly, walking away.

After a few rushed steps I came upon large glass windows and a single door leading into the library. I glanced out the glass and watched as the sun's rays kissed the land. Not good. Monsters worked best in the night. How long had I been studying? I turned my eyes back to the glass.

The college campus was well-manicured. A small fountain sat off to the left and the open street faced me. A large red bus pulled up to my building, huffing a loud sigh as it stopped. I took a deep breath, pushing down my fears, and threw open the door to exit the building.

I ran as fast as I could, glancing around, looking for enemies. What was safe? Home was compromised and I doubted staying on campus would protect me from the enemy that had attacked our home. I needed to get far away and head someplace where I could blend in. I entered the bus, swiped my card, and took a seat toward the back. I sat with my back facing the windows. I scanned the bus; it was nearly empty save for the bus driver and a mother and child sitting a few seats ahead of me. Just as the bus was about to pull off a man entered. He took the seat across from me and began using his cell.

Having finally collected all its passengers, the doors screeched closed and the worn-down bus chugged away from the campus. I leaned back in my seat, releasing a breath I didn't know I had been holding. Flicking open my cell phone, I dialed Dru again but the call went straight to voicemail. My heart sank low.

The bus continued its transit for several minutes before pulling to a stop on the opposite side of town. I stood up quickly and exited the bus. The mother and child shambled off behind me.

"Watch your step," the mother said to her son.

I made my way across the street, hitching my backpack higher. I needed to get to the local cafe, the Cat's Meow. It was Dru and I's meet up spot in case things got bad.

The Cat's Meow wasn't your typical cafe. Sure they served coffee and lattes, but did I mention that this cafe came with cats? I entered the cafe, a jingle of bells announcing my arrival, and quickly paid for an hour's worth of time. I took a seat at one of the back tables and tried Dru's cell once more.

Voicemail again.

An orange kitty ran its body against my legs and settled down on my feet to take a nap. I petted the cat, scratching between his ears. The cat arched its back in reply. I smiled lightly.

"Hey buddy," I said.

"Cute cat," a female voice said off to my right, "what's his name?"

"Tiger," I said without thinking. Tiger began to purr loudly.

"I suggest you leave here calmly, don't alert the staff or I will drain them all. Do we understand each other?"

I lifted my head, ceasing my petting. So they had found me. It was only a matter of time. Despite many years of dealing with creatures hunting me, I still couldn't hold back the shiver that ran down my spine. Tiger meowed and rubbed his head into my leg once more, begging for more love. I gave him one final pet and got up from my seat. I followed the stranger dressed all in black and exited the cafe. The woman led me down a nearby alleyway. Once she knew we were all alone, she retrieved a revolver from her hip holster, which sat nestled under her jacket. She pointed the firearm at my face.

"You move and I will put a bullet through your skull," she said.

"So what's your plan, you gonna make me stand out here all night?"

"You won't be using that smart mouth once backup comes."

Backup? I resisted the urge to smile. Looks like things were finally working out in my favor. I needed to act fast. I gave the woman a once-over. Vibrant natural red hair flowed down her face, stopping at her chest. Freckles dotted her face in an overwhelming pattern. She was thin and lanky, taller than me by six inches or so. Her blood red eyes stared at me harshly. She was a vampire, newly turned I reasoned. Her hand shook as she held the gun, which told me she wasn't used to killing. I decided I would take the gamble and fight her. First things first, I needed to get her angry. Distracting her was my ticket out of here.

"You need to work on your banter. I can tell you are not used to this," I said, smiling.

"My banter is just fine."

"You sound like a nerd trying to be cool and failing horribly."

"Shut up."

"Oh, nice retort. Come on, give me your best, I'm waiting."

"I said shut up!"

Yes, just a bit more.

"Wow. I can't believe they sent *you* to get me. That's just sad. I wonder what will happen if you fail. I saw a man get torn apart limb by limb once. Wasn't pretty."

"You don't know anything."

"Oh, I know that you are gonna go home empty handed."

"Shut up!" The red head exclaimed, lowering her gun just so slightly.

Bingo.

I concentrated hard on a single word, letting it reverberate through my mind: *sleep.* The vamp's eyes began to lower and she swayed lightly on her feet. I then focused all my energy into my palm and prayed that this would work. At first, nothing happened. I stood still, panic filling me. Then, slowly, my palms began to burn and a tingling feeling went through my arms and into my hands. A bright light filled the alley. The vamp screamed as the light cut into her skin, frying her. I willed the light away and collapsed to my knees. I took deep breaths and forced myself to rise. I made my way shakily to the vampire and glanced at her body which was burnt black. She lay on the ground gasping for air.

"Told you, you were going home empty handed."

I ran past her out of the alley, disappearing into the night.

✳✳✳

I spent the next two days in hiding. I had decided that living in plain sight was the safest way to go. I made a home on the corner of 3rd and 4th Streets. I sat on a blanket, one that I had picked up the night I ran into the vampire. No one really messed with me except for an elderly lady named Pam who, against my internal pleading, spent most of her time sitting beside me telling me stories of her late husband Harold. After two whole days of her non-stop chattering, I really felt like I knew the guy.

I checked my phone again, which I had charged in a nearby restaurant after buying a sandwich. No call from Dru. I sighed, pocketing my cell and turned my attention back to Pam.

"No call again?" she asked.

"No," I said, depression slowly sinking in.

"Maybe it's time to head home, this life doesn't suit you."

"I can't go home."

"Not safe?"

"You don't know the half of it."

"Oh I think I do, Nephilim."

Nephilim. A name I learned to hate. Nephilims were the cross of a human and angel. Our kind is rare, like ultra-rare, and those that exist are quickly hunted for their powers. Some are sold to be servants; some are killed for sport. Me, I was free, or at least I was until a few seconds ago.

I stood up quickly, a look of fear scrunching its way into my features. Pam grabbed my wrist, holding me in place.

"What do you want?" I asked.

"I'm not going to hurt you. I am here to deliver a message. I am a psychic."

I stared at her cautiously.

"Most people could never tell the difference between a human and a Nephilim, but your energy waves are different ever so slightly." Pam closed her eyes and her grip on my wrist tightened. "Return home, there you will meet your destiny. You will face many challenges, but if you bring down your walls, trust in another, then just perhaps you will survive."

I waited a moment but the psychic said nothing more.

"That's very vague."

Pam's eyes opened. "That's how it works. Can't give you all the answers, makes life boring that way. Now quickly go home and face your destiny."

Pam released my hand and stood up on wobbly feet. She walked away, not bothering to glance back. I pondered her words. Facing one's destiny sounded dangerous and deadly. Something I worked pretty hard on to avoid. If the psychic had found me, it would only be a matter of time before others would come by. I gathered all my items and began walking. That's when I felt my phone buzzing.

Dru's name played on the screen.

I flicked my finger across the screen answering the call. "Dru!"

"Harper, thank god."

"Dru, oh my god, You're okay."

"You must return home."

"But wasn't home compromised?" I asked.

"Please Harper, nowhere else is safe. I wouldn't be sending you there if it wasn't safe. Right, love?"

I paused, then said, "You're right, love."

"Good girl, now I scheduled an escort to collect you. They will collect you in eleven hours."

"The password?"

"'The wolf howls in the moonlight. And I nuzzle into the moon's embrace.' Please return home quickly."

"I'm on my way."

CHAPTER 3

SILAS

The first stop was the BPMI to collect my money. The BPMI or Bureau for the Prevention of Magical Interference was a large group that had agents of all kinds located around the world with the sole purpose of keeping magic and monsters a secret from the prying eyes of humans. Being a Dhampir meant that I was registered as a half human and that I could be taken down at any time if I turned to my vampiric roots. The BPMI's office was like any other regular building, with added monster corpses being shuffled in. The building was large and white, standing at five stories high. Around the back was a large loading dock where they brought in the corpses. Anyone looking in would assume this was just an office building and I guess that was the point. I pushed against the large glass doors leading inside.

"Silas," a voice rasped. I turned to the source of the noise. A plump receptionist sat behind a large oak desk off to my right. She smiled, running a hand through her graying hair. "What brings you in?"

"Just collecting pay," I said, approaching the desk. A disarray of trash, papers, and candy wrappers littered the surface. Hidden beneath the clutter was a name plaque reading "Leslie."

"Got a bounty did you?" She asked before being hit with a fit of harsh coughing. She placed her index finger in the air and kept it raised until her coughing died down. "Damn, cigs will kill ya, but I'll be damned 'cause they are good."

I nodded absentmindedly, pulling out a crumpled slip of paper from my back pocket. Leslie took the paper and pulled out thick-rimmed glasses. Her eyes moved rhythmically back and forth as she read. "And what exactly was the creature? Don't spare any details."

I relayed the information about my bounty to her. She stared at me smiling and wide-eyed behind her glasses. Once finished, she watched me carefully, assessing me. I must have passed because she looked away moments later and reached into a drawer. She pulled out a prefilled check and handed it to me. I pocketed the check, said my goodbyes, and left the building.

I made it down the stairs and around the block when I felt it. A predatory gaze. Every part of me groaned to bolt and run, to get as far away as possible, but I forced myself to stay calm. I was a predator, not prey. I closed my eyes, focusing on my surroundings and took a deep breath.

There. From my left. Whatever held me in, its gaze was moving fast. I forced my eyes open once more and took off at a sprint. I barely made it three steps when an arm shot out from my left. I twisted my body, avoiding the arm, and skidded to a halt. My brother, Lazarus, stood a few feet behind me. I stared at the man. His build was muscular, and he stood at a whopping six eleven. His raven hair was brushed to the left, partially hiding a large scar running through his left eye. I ducked, avoiding another attack, this time from my right. My other brother, Luther, identical minus the scar, stood in front of me blocking my path.

Their eyes bored into me. They each took a step and began running around me in lightning quick steps. I traced their movements, my head moving side to side. I'd seen this before, back when I used to practice fighting when I lived with Mother. It was hard to evade but not impossible.

The Twins skidded to a stop and with their extra momentum they shot out at me, fists blazing. I ducked and rolled to the side. Their fists slammed into one another with a crushing blow. If I hadn't moved in time, it would have been my head. In unison they pulled back their fists and looked over at me a good three feet away.

"We missed him," Luther said slowly.

"Again. Mother wants him," Lazarus said, equally as slow.

I didn't stick around to see what they had planned. I took off, heading down the street. The Twins appeared at my side almost instantly. They didn't reach for me, just ran beside me, matching my speed. I wasn't sure how long we ran like that. Racing down the streets, but soon I felt myself begin to slow. Running at full speed wasn't something I could do for long, half vampire or not. My lungs burned and with no more energy left I slowed to a stop. I doubled over, barely able to catch my breath. It took all my energy not to just collapse on the ground. They approached me from both sides. In a last ditch effort I pulled out my gun and aimed to my left.

A stinging pain seared through my right hand. My gun clattered to the ground. I looked around for the source of the pain and my breath caught in my throat. Anya, my older sister, stood behind me. A sleek black leather dress clung to her thin frame. Her equally dark stilettos clicked on the pavement as she made her way to me. Her skin, porcelain, stood out against the dark night. Her high cheekbones glinted in the light. She ran her hand through her silvery purple hair, her other hand gripping her sword.

"Sweet, dumb little brother, you're making this harder than it needs to be."

"Anya," I said, my voice barely louder than a whisper. I forced myself to ignore the searing pain in my wrist. Blood dripped down to the concrete below. The twins' eyes flashed red and they slowly began taking steps closer to me. I took a hesitant step back, feeling like a rabbit caught in the sights of wolves.

"Can we eat him?" Lazarus asked.

"Just a little bite?" Luther asked.

Anya closed the gap between us, placing her cold hand against my warm flesh. "You two know Mother's orders. We bring him back in one piece."

"But his blood—it's so delicious," one twin said, practically salivating.

"Can't you smell it?" The other asked, spit dribbling down his chin.

Anya emitted a sound that could only be described as a growl. "Your incompetence will get you killed one day."

Anya turned her attention to me. A devious smile crossed her lips. She launched her fist into my gut with strength that felt like a car had been rammed into my stomach. I doubled over unable to breathe. Black dots swam across my vision. I collapsed fully onto the ground, all my strength gone.

"Bring him to the car," Anya ordered.

Then darkness.

I couldn't move my body. This was a weird and startling feeling to have after waking up from being kidnapped by your half-siblings. I forced myself to focus on my surroundings rather than being overcome by fear. I was in a room. It was dark, but from what I could make out I was on a bed in the middle of the room. The space was pretty much empty besides a chair that sat across from the bed. I blinked my eyes slowly; whatever they had done to me was really kicking my ass. They must have drugged me. That would explain why I couldn't move and why I was so sluggish. A murmur echoed in the room.

I wasn't alone.

"Who's there," I asked, my voice barely a whisper.

Silence responded.

I waited for several minutes, the silence heavy in the air.

"You can't move."

I nearly jumped at the voice. It was quieter than a whisper, but my heart still beat fast in my chest. I forced myself to remain calm and tried speaking to the voice again.

"Who are you?"

"Why should I tell you?" The voice, female, hissed.

"I'm not going to hurt you."

"Clearly. You can't move."

She got me there. I tried pushing myself up into a sitting position. I managed it after several minutes. Something heavy clung to my left wrist, which I figured were handcuffs. My eyes had taken their time to adjust to the darkness and I could make out a figure sitting before me, mere feet away. How long had she been there?

"What's your name?" I tried once more.

"What's the point in telling you? My fate will be the same nevertheless."

"Why don't you escape?"

"*Idiota*. You think I would have left already if I could? I'm trapped just like you," she spat. The sound of jingling filled the air. She too, it appeared, was handcuffed.

"Why are you here?"

"You're a bigger idiota than I thought."

"You ever think that instead of insulting me we could help each other?"

"You're a monster, why would you help me?" she demanded. Her words hit me hard. A monster. That word was something I battled with my whole life and her words had sapped all the resistance I had built up against it. My head hung in shame. Whoever had captured her planned on using her for food. It was sickening. "Why do you look like someone just kicked your dog?"

I forced my feelings down. "We need to get out of here. Is there anything near you? Something we can use to pry open the handcuffs."

"No."

Of course there wasn't. Mother wouldn't have slipped up and left something that we could escape with in the room. I sighed lightly and turned my head toward the girl. I couldn't imagine what she was feeling. Being separated from the outside world just to be used as food. It was crazy and disheartening. She was probably scared out of her mind.

"My name is Silas." I paused trying to find the words. "I'm not one of them a … monster. I promise you. I will do everything in my power to get you out of here."

There was a long pause then, "You promise that? You'll help me get to my baby again?"

"Once I'm able to move. We'll figure a way out of this."

"My name is Ximena," she whispered.

"Oh, how cute." A voice spoke as the light switch was turned on. Blinding light filled the room. I used my free hand to cover my eyes. My movement was coming back to me. Mother entered into the room with refined grace. She was the spitting image of Anya, except her hair. While Anya's was a dyed purple, Mother's was a deep black. She had piercing red eyes and cheekbones that could cut glass. Her lips bore laugh lines and around her eyes held the beginning of small creases of crow's feet. Her pale hand rested on her hip, tapping against her beautiful red, crystal-adorned dress. Her eyes bored into me, eyebrows arched. "Silas. My dear baby boy. It's so good to have you home."

I wanted to tell her to fuck off, but my voice caught in my throat. There it was again—overwhelming fear. It had been ten years since I had last seen my mother, but here she was staring down at me like I was some pathetic ant under a magnifying glass. There was hunger in her eyes. She wanted me dead.

Mother draped her hand on my shoulder and smiled. My flesh burned against her cold touch. She moved her hand up my shoulder and grabbed my cheeks tightly. I wrestled to get free, but the drug was still heavy in my system. She pulled out a small vial and uncapped the bottle with her free hand. She forced my jaw open with amazing strength that no human had possessed and jammed the vial's contents down my throat.

Blood. It was blood. I gagged at the metallic taste, but Mother continued to hold me down. Blood coated my throat and, with nowhere else for it to go, I swallowed. A pang of pain ran through me. My heart felt like it was going to beat out of my chest. Mother released her hold on me. I collapsed onto the bed unable to move. It felt like every fiber of my being was screaming out. Burning searing pain flooded my senses. I couldn't breathe. Was I going to die?

"Isn't this glorious?" Mother shouted.

"What did you do to him?" I heard Ximena yell but she sounded so far away.

"I simply turned him into what he is meant to be. His true form."

I could feel myself slipping away. My humanity, something I had guarded for so long, had simply vanished. More blood filled my mouth, my own blood. My old canines fell onto the bed in a puddle of blood. New sharper deadlier canines burst from my gums. My eyes began to sting. A moan racked my body, followed by laughter. So this was what I was truly meant to be. I smiled, fangs gleaming. I looked to Ximena and launched at her, my body no longer paralyzed. I was nearly upon her when I felt a pull from my wrist. Damn handcuffs. I got down on all fours, taking in Ximena's scent—my prey. I felt a hand ruffle my hair. I looked up at Mother; she was smiling down at me, finally happy. I was her little monster.

"Behold Silas, Dhampir and next Prince of the Ravnos Clan," Mother declared. Ximena squirmed in her chair. I extended my arm toward her, but she was just out of my reach. I growled in rage, looking toward Mother. "Patience, little one you'll have your meal soon enough."

"Why would you do this? He's your son!" Ximena shouted.

"Precisely." Mother beamed.

"You're a monster!"

"You aren't wrong there." Mother smiled. "Oh Hell, I shouldn't let my little one go hungry. Go on and eat."

Mother undid the cuffs on my wrist. I looked to Ximena and was upon her before she could scream. My fangs found her throat. I pierced it and began to drink. Mouthful by mouthful. Ximena's struggles began to subside. Her once warm body turned cold. Her dark tan skin now ashen. My head began to clear, the blood lust disappearing. I looked down at my arms, covered in blood. Ximena's long straight raven hair was curled around my fingers. Her mouth hung open as if frozen in a permanent scream. Her eyes glazed over. Mother grabbed my shoulder, pulling me away from Ximena.

What have I done?

Everything I had worked so hard to preserve was gone in seconds. Mother pulled me into a hug. I stood there limply in her arms, unable to breathe.

"Your sins have been repaid," Mother whispered into my ear. Mother pulled away from me, rising to her feet. "Welcome to the other side."

CHAPTER 4

SILAS

I couldn't bear to look at Ximena's lifeless body. I wanted to crawl into a hole and die. I had killed her. Me. I had drained her of her blood and left nothing more than a husk. Mother had just left her body unceremoniously lying on the floor. I got off the bed and slowly approached the dead woman. Her soulless eyes stared up at me. I knelt down, placing my hands over her eyes, and closed them.

Guilt ate away at my gut. I had promised her that I would get her out of there and had not delivered, which cost Ximena her life. I bit back bile rising to my throat. I needed to get out of there, I needed a plan.

First things first, I needed to get out of the room. I approached the door and tried the knob. The door creaked open. *Strange, what was Mother planning? Does she want me to leave?*

I crept into the hallway. I had never seen this side of the Ravnos Manor. It must have been the new hall, under construction when I had left ten years ago. Wrestling with myself, I went left. I walked down another long hallway before entering a large room. It had a long table going down its length. Twenty six chairs sat resting under the table. The room was decorated in pelts and taxidermized animals. I walked past a stuffed bear standing at about six feet tall and went through another door.

I ended up in a kitchen. I walked down the aisle of countertops and large basin sinks. Another door greeted me at the end of the kitchen. I pushed the door open and stepped through. The smell of blood hung heavy in the air. Instinctively I went for my gun in my shoulder holster but wound up grabbing only air. The Twins stood in the middle of the room, a pile of bodies between them. Luther was holding a man by the throat, but froze in mid action as his eyes fell upon me.

"Look Brother …," Luther said.

"Our next meal is here," Lazarus said.

"We should eat him."

"Yes, we should."

I braced for the worst, but the worst never came.

Mother stood before me, her hair splattered with red. The Twins were standing still, mere inches from our mother. Lazarus released a choked sigh before he fell to his knees. He released a scream as one of his hands was severed from his body and tumbled to the ground. Luther stood in horror, backing away quickly. He nearly tripped on the pile of dead bodies him and his brother had drained just minutes before. Mother turned to face me and placed a cold clammy hand on my cheek. It felt wet against my skin.

"Boys," Mother called over her shoulder, "you'd better behave."

She smiled and turned away, walking past me. I felt myself release a shaky breath. I walked unsteadily past my brothers and through the next door, pulling it shut behind me. I slipped my hands into my pants pocket, but I couldn't stop them from shaking. Through the dim lighting my eyes caught a shadow drifting toward me. I braced myself. Anya approached but now was no longer in her skintight dress. She had traded it for a pair of black spandex pants and a white shirt with slits cut down the side revealing her black bra.

She attempted to make her way through the door I had just exited, but I stuck out my hand blocking her path. I hated my family, especially my sister, for dragging me back to this life, but I wasn't about to let her see what Mother had just done to her own brother. Anya's eyes went into slits. I stood fast to the spot, arm blocking her.

"Move aside Silas before I make you move," she said.

Sighing lightly, I moved my arm. Anya stepped past, opening the door. She looked inside and froze. She held the door open for five seconds then closed it. "Lazarus. Dumb bastard." She turned her attention to me. "Who cut off his hand?"

"Mother," I said, voice barely a whisper.

No emotion registered on her face. She blinked slowly and turned to go back where she had come from. I reached out and grabbed Anya's hand, but she shook it away.

"Follow me," she said, walking down the hallway. We ended up in what I could only call a living room. A sofa sat against a far wall facing a television. A reclining armchair sat diagonally from the couch. There was an end table next to the recliner with a cigarette tray and a folder resting on top. Anya retrieved the folder and passed it to me. I opened it, pulling out a small photo and one sheet of paper.

I looked at the photo intently, taking in all the details—something I had learned to do from my career in bounty hunting. It was of a woman with curly black hair. Her lips were full and housed two little dimples on each side of her smile. She wore thick black makeup around her honey brown eyes. She was thin and dressed in a purple crop top and jeans. Her right forearm showed a flowery tattoo as she held her hand up in a peace sign. Her toffee skin was dark in comparison to the woman she was next to. The woman next to her had her pale arm draped over the other woman's neck. Her lips were thin, and her hair was a deep brown that was cut in a pixie style. Her eyebrows were arched, and a ring poked out from under her nose. She wore a plain yellow dress. Her brownish red eyes stared back at me.

"Mother wants your bounty hunter experience. For the exchange of a bounty she'll let you go."

"A bounty?"

"I don't like repeating myself …" Anya said, annoyed. "The girl with the curls is Harper Beauregard. She took their last name and is the last surviving member of the Beauregard Clan out west. The Vampire beside her is her late Keeper, Ms. Drusilla Beauregard."

"Late?"

"Yes Mother found and killed Drusilla. Of course, she tortured the woman first. Exposed her to sunlight until she talked, and lucky for you she convinced Harper to meet back at the Beauregard Manor, in a few hours. Harper is not to be underestimated, she left behind a burnt vampire in her wake. Mother wants you to befriend her, earn her trust, then deliver her to the Ravnos Manor. Shouldn't be a problem for you, right?"

"Why me?" I asked, unable to believe my ears.

"Silas, you have something that none of our siblings do. Mother's affection. She treasures you and for some reason sees greatness in you."

"And yet she wants me dead," I said.

Anya rolled her eyes. "If Mother wanted you dead, you'd be six feet under."

I paused for a moment, then said, "Why does Mother want the girl?"

"She has something Mother wants."

"And I'm free? No more house calls?"

"You'll be as free as the day you left here ten years ago."

"Where was she last seen?"

"In a small town in Washington. North Haven."

CHAPTER 5

SILAS

Being stuck in a plane really gives you time to think.

And I really hated that.

Time to think, in this case, meant the guilt of sacrificing someone else for myself. My conscience was being put through the wringer. I sat at the window gazing out, watching the shapeless clouds go by. Harper, whoever she was, was just an average girl whose life was about to be flipped upside down. I didn't know why Mother wanted her or what she hoped to gain, but it couldn't be anything good.

Was I doing the wrong thing?

I sighed, leaning my head against the window. I was leading a woman to her death and Mother expected me to gain the girl's trust on top of all that. I shook my head swiftly.

I needed to survive.

Since the day I was born I had always been looking out for myself. Why start doing differently now?

"No more house calls," I whispered to myself. "Do this one thing and you are free."

The plane landed some hours later. I exited the airport and was greeted by a sweet red Rolls-Royce Wraith. I let loose a whistle and approached the car. Mother sure liked to do things in style. I opened the door and ran my hand against the real leather interior.

"Damn she's a beaut."

I entered the car and sped off down the street, leaving skid marks behind me.

***

Beauregard Manor was different from Ravnos. Where Ravnos Manor was one building decorated with the most elegant treasures, Beauregard was a collection of run-down apartments. I went up to the apartments and down a row of doors exposed to the sunlight. If I remembered correctly from the file, Harper's room was on the first floor, unit A6. I came across her door and couldn't help but stare. It was covered in stickers, most of them about female empowerment, some of them funny. I particularly like the "Drink Coffee, Hail Satan" one. I knocked and placed my ear against the black wood, listening.

A scream answered back.

"Shit," I said, backing up. I placed my foot against the door and began kicking. At first the door didn't give but after some persuasion the wood around the knob began to splinter. A loud crack sounded and the door buckled, allowing me access inside. I slipped past and entered a large living room.

Standing in the center was Harper and facing her was a polar bear. It was a peculiar sight, but it wasn't the first time I had seen a Shifter. Shifters—or humans with the magical ability to turn into an exact copy of one animal—weren't too hard to kill. Most Shifters took on the form of a wolf or big cat, some even took on the form of house pets. They were actually pretty low on the danger scale, but a bear, well, that was going to be its own battle.

The bear rose on its hind legs and Harper backed away quickly, toppling over a television in the process. I withdrew my gun from its shoulder holster and fired at the bear. The bullet caught the massive beast in the neck. Blood spurted out from its flesh, and it turned its large head in my direction.

Its eyes locked on me and narrowed. Instead of wounding the creature I had only managed to piss it off. Great.

The bear charged. I stood my ground, firing more shots. The bullets struck the bear in the chest, but the beast ignored them, not slowing down. At the last second, I jumped to the side to avoid becoming a pancake. Before I could rise, the bear careened toward me again, slamming its massive paw into my side. I was lifted off my feet and from the momentum I flew about six feet straight into wall. I landed in a heap on the ground.

Damn, that hurt.

I groaned lightly and attempted to stand. The sound of footsteps squeaked as Harper took off running, her shoes catching on the linoleum. Just as she was out the door another bear came into the apartment, this one a brown bear. Harper stopped in her tracks and began backing away.

I needed to get to Harper. I forced myself to my feet. The polar bear crept closer, forcing me to move backwards. Harper continued moving back as well and in seconds our backs touched.

"They aren't friends of yours, are they?" Harper asked.

"I work alone," I said.

"Ah. Gotcha. So why are you here?"

"I'm your escort. You wouldn't happen to have any other weapons, would you? I dropped my gun when Teddy here hit me."

"I can get weapons, I just need you to distract … both bears."

I sighed. "Okay. Go for it. Just be careful."

Shifters had the mind of a human whenever they were in their animal form, making them a dangerous enemy if they thought primarily with their human brains. A regular animal could be dangerous, but an animal with a human mind was something you didn't want to mess with. They had many weaknesses but the one thing that really wounded them was they also had the instincts of their animal counterpart. So take for example any predator with a prey drive, as in our bear friends. Sure, they were thinking with their human brains but simply running would kick their brains into bear mode, forcing them to follow me without thought. It would take them a few seconds for their human brains to regain control, thus buying Harper some time to get weapons. It was a dangerous plan, but what choice did we have?

I took a deep breath, raised my arms over my head shouting, "Hey you stupid bears! Follow me!"

I broke out in a sprint, rushing out the doors—and just as I planned the two bears' animal instincts took over and they followed, leaving Harper alone in the apartment. I was at my car in seconds and by then the bears slowed their pace. Shit, their human brains were gaining control. I eyed the apartment desperately.

Where the hell was Harper? She could've left me for all I know, made her escape while I foolishly fought the Shifters unarmed. Then the brown bear released a yelp and stood up on its hind legs. It swung around, revealing the hilt of a blade in its shoulder with Harper holding on for dear life.

Harper managed to slip her hand into her waist band and threw my Glock near me. I retrieved the gun just as the polar bear crashed into me. I hit the car hard, bouncing off and landing on the ground in a painful heap. Somehow I still managed to hold on to my gun. I held it more firmly in my hand and pointed it at the polar bear's skull. I fired a shot, hitting it right between the eyes. The bear stood still for a moment before crashing to the ground with a loud thump.

Its fellow companion, the brown bear, ceased its movements for a moment, looking at its fallen comrade. Then it threw Harper off its back and barreled into the woods. Harper stood up slowly and began dusting herself off. I too forced myself to my feet and began making my way to her.

She reached into her waistband once more, retrieving another gun. She pointed it at me, hands shaking.

I took a step forward. "You don't want to shoot me. Drusilla sent me. The wolf howls in the moonlight."

Harper peered around the gun but didn't lower it. Damn, had Anya given me the wrong password? I took another step forward and, in response, Harper positioned her aim at my head.

"Stay back," she said.

I took another step toward her and in one fluid action grabbed the gun by the muzzle, palm resting over the barrel. "The wolf howls in the moonlight."

She looked at me in amazement, then said, "And I nuzzle into the moon's embrace."

"Good girl," I said pocketing the gun.

"How'd you know I wasn't going to shoot you?"

"Fat chance you would have. You left the safety on," I said. Heat rose to her cheeks. She slipped her hands into her pockets and rocked back on her feet. "We need to leave. It's only a matter of time before others come looking for you. As Drusilla ordered, I am to take you to a safe house in Sable."

"Sable?"

"Yes. That is where Dru has arranged to meet you."

She nodded and began walking past me. Harper was a small girl, about five foot two, but she was brave. She stood up against a stranger and two bear shifters, something most people would have cut and run. Despite wanting to keep things strictly business, I was thoroughly impressed.

Harper entered the car on the passenger's side and began buckling up. I nodded my head, very impressive indeed.

***

The drive through North Haven was a quiet one. I drove all night and into the early morning until we found a motel where Harper felt safe. I paid for the one-bedroom and collapsed onto the bed. Harper sat down on the edge of the other bed, staring at the floor.

"So we need to talk," Harper said, turning to face me.

"Yeah."

"Who are you?"

"As I said earlier, Drusilla sent me to take you to her safe house in Sable."

"You know, it's just weird because Dru never mentioned a safe house," she said skeptically.

"It wouldn't be safe if she blabbed to everyone about it, now would it?"

Harper paused. I glanced over at her, her face conflicted. Moments of silence ticked by.

"What's bothering you?" I asked.

"Why should I trust you not to slit my throat when I sleep?"

"If I wanted you dead, I would've killed you while we were alone at the apartment. Or even easier, let the bears eat you."

Harper swallowed, eyes growing wide.

"But I don't intend to kill you," I said.

Harper released a sigh. "I can't sleep with you … here … in this room. I don't even know you. I can't trust you."

"Look, I'm not going to hurt you or anything. I'm just going to sleep. If you plan to stay up all night, that's on you, but I'm going to bed."

There was a long pause, then Harper fell back onto the bed and placed her forearm over her eyes. I looked away and felt a pang of hunger hit me. I needed blood. Whether I liked to admit it, I needed blood to heal, and it would only be a matter of time before I lost control. I swallowed the bile rising in my throat. I leaned over the edge of the bed, picking up my backpack. I dug through it and pulled out a small bag of blood. Harper sat up at the sound of my searching. She peered at me with curious eyes.

"I knew it," she said. "You're a Dhampir!"

"Yeah okay, keep your voice down."

"I've never met a Dhampir before, I heard your kind are very rare."

I nodded my head and pierced the bag of blood with one of my fangs. I took a sip and nearly gagged as the metallic tang hit my taste buds. I thought having my vampiric side awakened would lead me to actually like the taste of blood. I forced myself to take another sip. Harper peered at me from across the room.

"Can I help you?" I asked with irritation pecking at me.

"It's just so interesting. I mean what's it like?"

"What's what like?"

"Drinking blood."

"It tastes like crap."

"Hmm ... have you always had to drink blood?"

I sighed as a small dribble of blood ran down my lip. "No. I haven't," I answered simply.

"So why now?"

"I just do," I said, wiping away the blood.

"But why?"

"Does it matter! I need the blood to heal, end of story. Now turn in for the night, we have a long drive ahead of us."

Harper frowned and lay back down. She turned her back to me. Minutes went by and just when I thought she was finally asleep I heard her whisper. "Um ... Dhampir?"

"What?" I whispered.

"What's your name?"

"Silas," I said, letting the darkness take me.

CHAPTER 6

HARPER

I couldn't sleep.

I sat up in bed quietly so as to not wake the sleeping Dhampir. I glanced his way; he didn't appear to be so menacing when he was knocked out. His raven bangs blanketed his eyes, and his olive skin was covered lightly with sweat. He tossed and turned in his sleep, mouth opening as if to scream.

"Ximena," he whispered.

I got up from bed, crossed the room, and stood before Silas. Nephilim and angels had many powers, our most dangerous being mind manipulation. If in good hands it could be used to help heal, but in the wrong hands, mind control could break a person's psyche permanently.

Delicately, I placed my fingertips on his forehead. His eyes fluttered at my touch, but before he could wake, I whispered the word *sleep* in my mind. His breathing became deeper, and he ceased his tossing and turning. The spell I had put him under would guarantee a good night's sleep, free of nightmares.

"You're welcome," I said quietly.

What was a man like him afraid of? What creatures had he come across and what had left their mark? I walked back over to my bed. Sighing, I plopped down on the edge. Then there was a light clink, the sound of something small, but hard, hitting glass. I cautiously crept toward the window. Grabbing a single strip of the blinds, I flicked it open peering outside.

A pair of golden brown eyes stared back at me.

I stifled a yell and fell backward, tripping over my bag, landing in a crumpled mess. My heart beat wildly in my chest. I waited, but nothing happened. No raining down of glass or monsters jumping through the window. I got to my feet approaching the window again. I pulled down the blinds once more and glanced outside.

My breath caught in my throat.

"Mom," I said in disbelief.

I shut the blinds and quickly threw on my jacket. I went to the motel room door and grasped the doorknob. I glanced back at Silas, still soundlessly sleeping, and opened the door. The cold assaulted me instantly, but I barely felt it as I came face-to-face with my mother.

Mom was a beautiful woman. Her angelic radiance shined through the body she had been in possession of. Due to constantly switching bodies over the years, she looked a little bit different every time I saw her, though she tried to keep up with a trend. African American women. This body had nice evenly tanned skin clear of imperfections, a smile that housed a small dimple, bright brown eyes, and her hair, this time, was done up in chunky box braids.

Mom flashed her perfect smile at me and pulled me into a tight hug. I hugged her back, tears escaping my eyes. At the feeling of my hot tears, she pulled away and took my face in her hands.

"Harper," she whispered, "you've grown into a beautiful young lady."

"Where have you been? How have you been? God, mom, it's been three years."

"I know." She pulled me into a tight hug. "And I'm afraid this might be the last time we see each other again."

"What do you mean?" I asked, fear filling my mind.

"Just like you, my kind is being hunted. The demons grow bold and have been killing angels. My kind has been forced to go into hiding as the only way to preserve our species. There are only a select few angels who fight back."

"Mom, I had no idea. If I had known…"

"There was nothing you could have done. I'm afraid I have a target on my back. One from which I cannot escape. I came to say goodbye."

"Mom, don't talk like that. We can fight this together."

"The demons are ruthless. The last thing I want is for them to find my Nephilim child."

"I can't just let you go …"

"Harper …" Mom placed her hands on my shoulders. "There is so much I wanted to do for you. So much I wanted to say."

"Then say it to me as we leave here together."

"I'm sorry, Harper. I'm sorry I made your life like this. Putting you in danger all just for being what you are. I'm sorry I couldn't have been more of a mother to you. I wish I'd had more time."

She paused, reaching into her pocket. She pulled out a bracelet made up of small rocks. She took my right hand pulling up my sleeve, revealing my flower tattoo. She placed the bracelet around my wrist, securing it. "These stones were made from rocks in the garden of Eden. I had it specialty crafted to help amplify your powers. Only use it in times of dire need."

"Mom …"

"Remember the first time you used your powers?"

"Why bring that up now?" I asked.

Mom laughed lightly. She placed her fingertips on my forehead. One second I was in a dingy motel parking lot, the next I was on a playground. Mom stood next to me, her body was see-through with a glowing hue around her. I reached out a hand to her and realized I too was see-through.

"What's going on?" I said, panicked.

"Don't worry honey, it's only a vision."

I looked around, taking in my surroundings. Close by was a bright red slide, the kind that when you slid down it, you would get electrocuted. Not too far off were a pair of monkey bars and swings. Black mulch lined the ground. I walked over to the slide and reached out a hesitant hand. My fingers went right through. I pulled my hand out of the slide and stared in awe.

I heard a series of giggles from behind. Four children ran through my legs, all playing tag. They ran past the swing where a lonely girl sat. She wasn't swinging, just sitting. And it wasn't just any girl—it was me. A much younger me, about six years old. My hair was a wild mess of black curls. I was also short for my age, wearing a pair of overalls and a bright green t-shirt. My mother, who also appeared younger, was crouched down in front of me, her hand holding on to mine.

I approached the pair, walking slowly.

"Harper, what's wrong?" My younger mom asked.

"I'm scared." My younger self confessed.

"Oh Harper, there's nothing to be afraid of. They are just human children."

"But ..."

My younger mother took my younger self's hand and guided her to the group of children playing tag. She stopped in front of the group, disrupting their game.

"Hello. My daughter Harper is very shy but she wanted to join in your game of tag. Would that be ok?"

One of the girls with golden yellow hair smiled and reached out a hand, touching my younger self's shoulder.

"You're it!" The girl shouted.

A smile grew across my younger self's face, and she began chasing after the children. They played like that for quite some time, chasing each other and laughing. Making up ridiculous rules that made no sense, but all in the name of fun.

I took a seat in the mulch, watching my younger self. She was so carefree. I couldn't help but feel a little jealous. I couldn't remember the last time I wasn't scared. I had been on the run for so long. What must it have felt like to grow up with a normal life? To not be hunted or sought after because of what you are.

An ice cream truck's song called out, stopping the kids dead in their tracks. Each child ran to their respective parent and begged for the frozen delight. A group of parents and children filed around the truck each placing their order. One by one the ice cream was handed out until it was my younger self's turn.

"Mommy, can I have a scoop of strawberry?" I asked with a gleam of hope in my innocent eyes.

"Of course," my younger mother said.

My younger mom placed our order and the man in the ice cream truck began scooping. My younger self looked at all her new friends, each enjoying their treats. My younger mother handed the ice cream over to my younger self and she joined the group of children.

My younger self began to eat the strawberry ice cream with a look of pure happiness on her face. Her friend with the golden yellow hair, who she had come to know as Delsea, sat next to her, chocolate dribbling down her chin.

A shrill scream rang out from behind the group of children. Everyone's gaze turned to a man who wore a beat-up band tee and jeans. He was missing a shoe and blood dripped down from his head. His skin was ashen and one of his eyes hung outside his head, attached to a single stringy piece of flesh.

Delsea screamed. The man whipped his head around toward the sound and began running toward us. The parents and children all screamed. Hurriedly the parents snatched up their children, running away. My younger mother glanced at my younger self and ran forward, meeting the zombie halfway. She began to fight the beast, a blade of pure light in her hands. My younger self watched on in horror and fear.

A black swirling portal opened. Immediate heat hit me and my younger self gasped. A woman stepped out from the black. Her buzzed and dyed white hair stood out against her crimson tan skin. Beautiful black makeup coated her eyes and full lips. She wore a dark dress that went down to her mid-thigh. Rams' horns protruded painfully from her skull. Her eyes, black pools lacking any white, stared at me and Delsea.

Delsea screamed once more, looking around. Tears ran down her cheeks. "Mama!"

Delsea's mother did not respond. My younger self turned around looking at the crumpled form of Delsea's mother who had passed out from the shock. Delsea kneeled and grabbed her mother's hand and began shaking her desperately.

"Please wake up Mama!"

The woman from the shadows began approaching my younger self and Delsea. My younger self grabbed Delsea's other hand trying to lead her away but the girl stayed put. Though I feared for my younger self and the girl, there was nothing I could do, just watch on in silence. I turned around quickly, watching as my younger self glanced between Delsea and the demon. My younger self stepped in front of her friend with her palms out.

The demon smiled and brought fire to her hands, slowly approaching.

"Harper!" My younger mother screamed, still fighting the zombie.

My younger self gulped and closed her eyes. A bright light washed over the entire park, blinding all who stood in its sublime glow. People screamed, clutching at their faces. Then just as soon as it had come the light faded, disappearing back into my younger self's hands. My younger self opened her eyes and the demon stood before her, mere inches away. Her hands no longer burned fire. Dark blood dripped down the woman's eyes and, before she could move, my younger mother used her heavenly light blade to lop off her head.

The demon's body crashed to the ground and her head rolled onto my younger self's shoes. My younger self wiped at her face, smearing away dark blood.

"Monster!" Delsea shouted at my younger self. "You're one of them!"

My younger mother picked up my younger self and quickly left the park, leaving Delsea and the other children in the past.

The world around me turned white and I was standing once more in the motel parking lot. Mother stood before me, a frown on her face.

"I'm sorry you had to relive that," she said.

"Why did you show me?"

"Harper," my mom began, "you have spent the last years of your life hiding who you were, you've forgotten how powerful you truly are. There will come a time where you will trust someone enough to tell them your secret. Promise me, when that time comes you will not run away."

"Mom, they will think I'm a monster. Just like Delsea did."

"Harper, promise me," she said, a look of desperation on her face.

I nodded and she pulled me into another hug. She kissed my cheek lightly. I held on to her tightly, too afraid of letting her go. My mom was the first to break our hug. She took a few steps back, unfurling her large black wings, which were hidden beneath the skin of her shoulder blades. The wind picked up around me as she flapped her wings and slowly lifted to the sky.

"You have such great power and a heart made of gold. Don't forget that sweetie."

"Mom, I *will* see you again."

"I hope so, and when I do, you will get an earful about that tattoo," she smiled and then disappeared into the night.

The smile faded from my face. I was alone again. Truly alone. My heart grew heavy and I couldn't stop the tears from flowing free. I don't know how long I stood there like that, but eventually I went back into my motel room, throwing off my jacket and shoes. I glanced over at Silas, who was still asleep, and clambered into bed. I was exhausted and it wasn't too long before I too was asleep.

CHAPTER 7

SILAS

I woke up feeling like I got hit by a train, which for all intents and purposes I pretty much did when a one-ton bear barreled into me the day before. I was sore all over but feeling much better comparatively. That blood must have really done the trick. I sucked in a deep breath and sat up. The world swam around me, and it took all my energy to keep from puking. I glanced over at the other bed and found the sleeping form of Harper, just where I had left her. I released a sigh, letting my nerves escape.

Against my better judgment, I stood up and slowly made my way to the bathroom. I locked the door behind me and stared into the mirror. God, I looked hellish. I made my way to the shower, turned it on blasting hot, and stepped in. I let the roaring water wash over my aching body and stood there for some time, just lost in the moment. Then the thoughts started to creep in. What did my mother want with Harper? Shifters were after her too which meant whatever Harper was involved in, it wasn't isolated.

There was a knock at the door. Then Harper's voice. "Silas, are you almost done in there? I have to pee."

I rolled my eyes and turned off the water. I grabbed a fluffy towel and stepped out of the shower. I wrapped the towel around my waist and opened the bathroom door. Cold air greeted me, and I had to resist the urge to close the bathroom door again. Harper shuffled past into the bathroom, pulling the door close behind her. I walked over to my bag, pulled out a fresh pair of boxers, and slipped them on. The shower screamed from inside the bathroom. I quickly got dressed and packed up my things. We needed to hit the road as soon as possible. It would only be a matter of time before other Shifters caught up with us.

Harper exited the bathroom a short while later, dressed in only a towel. I averted my eyes and faced the door as she got dressed. I could hear her shuffling about, opening her bag, and moving fabric over her flesh. Had my hearing gotten better? I brushed it off and without thinking turned to face Harper. She screamed, raised her hand over her breast, and turned to face the other wall. Heat rose to my cheeks.

"Shit, sorry," I said, turning around again. "I thought you were done."

"Are you some kind of pervert!"

"No. I really thought you were done. Sorry."

A few seconds went by, and I resisted the urge to turn around once more. Harper zipped her bag shut and the sound of more fabric brushing against skin filled the air once again. She took a deep breath and said, "You can look now."

I hesitantly turned around to face Harper dressed in jeans, a Captain America belly shirt, and a leather jacket. She slipped her feet into her sneakers and grabbed her bag, not looking at me. Red burned her face.

"I really am sorry," I said, not making eye contact.

"It's fine. I don't think you really got a good look," she said. Perfect perky brown breasts the size of oranges, with dark brown nipples filled my mind. I brushed the thought away.

"Nope, I barely saw them," I said a little too fast. "Anyway, we need to focus on leaving."

She nodded and shouldered her bag. "I'm ready when you are."

I exited the motel room with Harper following close behind. We entered the car. Harper pulled out her polaroid camera and snapped a picture of me. I stared at her for a moment as the picture printed.

"What was that for?" I asked.

"I want to document this road trip. Dru and I planned on taking a road trip next month. I can't wait to see her and show her the photos. She always encouraged me to take photos, she said I was really great at it. Now …" She trailed off.

I looked at her for a moment and put the car in reverse. "Well … I get it. I guess you can take as many pictures as you want," I said, backing up. We traveled down the long stretch of road in silence for several minutes. My mind screamed at me to speak, but I bit my tongue. Finally, Harper broke the silence.

"So Si. Tell me a little bit about yourself."

"Si?" I asked, raising an eyebrow.

"You know, short for Silas."

I sighed and switched lanes. "What do you want to know?"

"How old are you?"

"Why don't you take a guess? It might pass the time."

"Thirty."

"Wrong."

Harper frowned, her face twisting in concentration. "Thirty-two."

"Nope."

"Thirty-one."

"Lower."

"Twenty-eight."

"Ding ding. You win the prize."

"Oh, and what's that?"

"A nice, scenic view of Washington State."

"Si. It's pouring buckets."

I smiled and turned my eyes back to the road. Dread swam through me. I couldn't allow myself to get close to my target. After all, in a matter of days, she'd be Mother's property. Mother could do what she wished with her. Torture, maiming, or even killing—was it really worth my freedom?

Time began to slow. Mother's eerily smiling face flashed through my mind. My heart began to race. I couldn't breathe. I tried to suck in air, but nothing touched my lungs. I held the wheel in an ironclad grip. Harper placed her hand on my shoulder.

"Are you alright?" She asked.

Time sped up again. "Yeah, I'm fine. Just need some coffee."

"There's a Starbucks at the next exit," she said, pointing to a sign.

I nodded and pulled off on the exit ramp.

***

I took a sip of my vanilla iced coffee as I pulled out of the drive-thru. Sweet liquid splashed down my throat and I welcomed its cold embrace. It sure beat drinking blood. Harper swirled the straw through her frappe and licked off the excess whipped cream. She wrapped her arm around my shoulder as I pulled up to a stop sign. She held her polaroid in her free hand and snapped a selfie of the two of us. The picture printed and Harper held the frame in between her fingertips, shaking the photo. I pulled away from the stop sign.

"This is definitely one for the picture books," she said, slipping the now-developed picture into a folder in her bag.

I leaned back in my seat as I pulled back onto the freeway. I focused on the road putting miles behind us.

Harper retrieved her headphones from her bag and slipped them over her head. Seconds later music boomed through her headphones, and I could make out every word. I tapped her on the shoulder and she took off her headphones, looking at me quizzically.

"You might as well just play your music. I can hear every word," I said.

She nodded and seconds later soft music played in the car. It was a new song I had never heard before.

"What's the name of that song?"

"'The Bones.' It's my new obsession," she said, smiling. Her head bobbed to the beat and she hummed along. After the song had finished Harper turned to face me. "So tell me more about you. I mean we do have three days to get to know each other, you know, before we get to the safe house."

"What do you want to know?"

"Hmm …" she said, placing her index finger to her temple. "So how did you know Dru?"

Shit. That was a loaded question. *How do I explain that? I mean, hey I'm basically here to escort you to your doom. Don't think she'd like that answer. No, I need to stick to the truth as best as I can so I don't get tangled up in a lie.*

"I don't really know Drusilla. I was just hired by her."

"Dru hired a complete stranger?" Harper said, her face perplexed.

"My mother knows Dru. So I'm not exactly a complete stranger."

Nice recovery. Now to steer this conversation somewhere else.

"So, I have a question for you Harper."

"Shoot."

"How did a human like you get into the vampiric world?"

Harper glanced out the windshield and sighed. "I never like telling this story, but since we are getting to know each other, I'll make an exception. So, it all started five years ago. I was failing all my classes, not because I was stupid, but because I just didn't care anymore. I decided to just drop out of college. I felt so lost at that point. I grew up with my grandfather and he wanted to see me graduate, but I just couldn't do it. I felt this terrible pain of guilt. It ate away at me every day, so I decided to end that pain, even if it was just temporary. I started going to bars and drinking all night. Then one night I met this man. He was the definition of tall, dark, and handsome."

"Is that really a thing?"

"Yes," she said with irritation in her voice.

"Continue," I said apologetically.

"Anyway, he came up to me and we started talking. I remember that he had led me out of the bar and into his car, said he wanted to show me something, and I was so drunk I followed him."

I glanced over at Harper; she stared down at her hands, unwilling to make eye contact.

"We got into the car and he drove off and took me to this secluded place. At that point, I started sobering up pretty fast.

He parked the car and reached for me with this inhuman speed. He grabbed me by the neck, and I swear his grip was so hard he nearly crushed my windpipe. Then he bit me."

"Shit."

"He was a vampire and I had stupidly become his meal. That's when he started undressing me. He ripped off my shirt and began to …"

"You don't have to tell me anymore Harper."

She crossed her arms over her chest. Her eyes were squeezed shut and her chest heaved.

"Harper …" I began.

"I'm not sure how long he fed on me but soon I felt this tearing pain and the vamp was yanked off of me. I remember screaming and seeing this woman. It turned out to be Dru. She had saved me. Dru subdued the vamp and came to my aid. She took off her jacket and covered me. Then I lost consciousness. I remember waking up in a bed all alone. That's when Dru came in."

A small smile graced her lips.

"She told me that the man would no longer hurt me and that I would need to recover from all the blood loss. The room became my home over the next couple of days. Dru respected me and kept her distance, but I started to fall for her. She was kind, caring, and introduced me to the world of Vampires." Harper sucked in a small breath.

"She told me I didn't have to return to my old life, that I could stay with her and she would become my Keeper in exchange for a fresh supply of my blood. I was so scared when she offered me that, you know? I mean here was a monster from legend actually real and she wanted me, but I knew deep down I wanted her too. So I decided to stay and up until recently, I had started getting my life on track.

Started going back to school and even planned a trip to visit my grandfather with Dru. I planned on asking her to be my girlfriend, but then …"

Tears flowed down Harper's cheeks.

I glanced over at her unsure of what to do. I had never been around people that cried. I mean, some of my bounties cried, but that was because their life was about to end. I didn't need to comfort them. So I did the only thing I could think of. Something I had seen in some movie a chick had dragged me to.

"Hey, hey. Don't cry." I pulled over to the side of the road.

"I mean, I've been through a lot with Dru. I just miss her …"

"Dru is so proud of you," I said, wrapping an arm around her shoulder.

"You really believe that?"

"Of course. Harper, you stood up against two Shifters yesterday and you haven't lost that chipper smile of yours."

Harper sniffled and wiped at her eyes. "Thanks, Si."

I nodded, pulling back onto the highway. We sat in silence for a moment before Harper spoke again.

"So what's it like?"

"What?" I asked, switching lanes.

"Being a Dhampir. I imagine it must be scary."

I sighed, "It's … I don't know."

"Let me rephrase. What can you do that a vamp can't?"

"Well … I can't fly for starters," I said, suppressing a laugh.

"Can you move as fast?"

"Not as fast, but I am pretty fast in my own right. I also have more endurance and strength than the average human."

"I noticed that your eyes change color."

"Yeah, they do that."

"So is it true? That a Dhampir has to awaken their powers by drinking blood first?"

I paused, feeling the guilt tear through me. "Yeah, it's true, Dhampirs don't really have any powers, just small things like a more acute sense of smell, but they don't get their full range of abilities until they kill," I said, my voice barely a whisper.

"Silas …"

"It's fine. I only gained my powers not too long ago."

"I'm sorry. I shouldn't have said anything."

"Her name was Ximena. I only met her once but … I promised her …"

I glanced down at the wheel. Harper took my hand in hers and squeezed.

"We all make mistakes. We have to learn to accept that."

I hoped she was right, that one day the guilt would pass and I could live a normal life. I squeezed her hand back and continued onward.

CHAPTER 8

SILAS

I awoke to a suspicious noise.

We had logged several hours on the road previously and when I didn't have any more consciousness left, I pulled off the freeway into a hotel a mile from the exit. We got a room and went to sleep, but not too long after I heard the sound.

To anyone else, it was nothing too out of the ordinary, just a light scratching sound. I sat up and listened. It continued. To my sensitive ears it was like nails on a chalkboard—and it was getting closer. I got out of bed as quietly as possible and slipped into my boots. I approached Harper's bed and placed my hand over her mouth. She jumped. I placed my index finger on my lips and pointed to her shoes. Harper nodded and went to work putting on her shoes and backpack. I reached for my bag, pulling out my gun and silencer. I secured both together and threw Harper a gun of her own. She did the same and cradled the pistol to her chest. I motioned for her to stand behind me.

I held my gun ready to fire. My heart beat loudly in my chest. The lock on the doorknob twisted open and I approached slowly. Harper began to follow, but I motioned for her to stay still. The door was pushed open but stopped when the locked chain caught. A black clawed hand reached into the door, fiddling with the lock. I slammed the door on the hand and a yowl filled the air. I held the door against the hand, hearing it crunch under the pressure.

Suddenly the door was flung open with extreme force, ripping the chain from the wall. I threw my hands up, blocking the raining wood. I misstepped and fell backward, landing in a heap away from Harper. Miraculously, I had somehow managed to hold on to my gun. I sat up quickly and saw that facing us was an African Werewolf. Unlike its cousin, the American Werewolf, this one had the face of a pharaoh hound. Its body was long and sleek. A tuff of hair was poised on its head, and it had a long skinny tail that twitched lightly as it walked. It favored its right paw as it strolled into the room. It sniffed at the air, taking in deep breaths. Its sights landed on Harper. The beast bounded toward her. Harper fired her gun once before it was upon her. I hopped to my feet and grabbed the monster by the neck, yanking the creature away from Harper.

I fired one shot into the beast's dome and the creature instantly went still. I dropped the creature onto the floor as the wretched scent of its blood filled my nostrils. I gagged and slammed my hand over my nose.

Harper pointed behind me, her hand shaking. "We've still got company."

I turned to face three more Werewolves all creeping toward us slowly, fangs glinting. I backed farther into the room. Harper ran for the balcony's sliding glass door and threw it open. She ran outside and began climbing over the balcony fence. The first werewolf charged. It went straight for my shin. I leaped back and aimed my gun at its head. Just as I was about to fire, another werewolf tackled me from the side. I landed on the ground hard. The third barreled over me and went straight for Harper.

I aimed my gun for the werewolf going after Harper but fangs sunk into my arm. I resisted the urge to scream as the beast chomped down harder. My grip on my gun slipped and the 9mm clacked onto the ground. The second werewolf circled around me, then went after Harper. The werewolf taking a chunk out of my arm pulled me toward it. Using my free hand, I sent a punch into the werewolf's eye. Its hold loosened and I pulled my arm free. I scrambled across the floor, reaching for my gun. The werewolf charged once again. I grasped my Glock and rolled onto my back, firing a single round.

The werewolf slid to a stop at my feet, its breath ragged. I forced myself to stand and fired a shot at the two remaining werewolves who were perched on the balcony. Harper had since climbed over the balcony railing and was desperately hanging on to the cold metal bars. I hit one werewolf square in the shoulder. The other werewolf jumped in front of its injured brethren. It rose to its hind legs. That's when something grabbed my ankle. I was yanked off my feet and sent crashing to the floor below; my gun escaped my grip and slid into the darkness. A human hand with an iron grip held me down. The man once werewolf placed another hand on my leg. His hand began to contort and shake, quickly turning into a werewolf paw. His claws dug into my flesh. A flash of pain shot through me as blood trickled down my leg. The werewolves on the balcony paused, turning their attention to me.

"Shit," I whispered.

"Such an exquisite scent," the wolfman holding me said.

The two werewolves abandoned their post and crept toward me. I glanced toward the balcony railing; Harper was nowhere to be seen. *Shit, has she fallen to her death? After all, we're on the fifth floor. Then again, I didn't hear a thud or even a scream for that matter.* I turned my attention back to the wolfman and sent a kick to his face.

"Let. Me. Go," I said with each kick.

The wolfman's hand loosened and I yanked my ankle free. The other two would be upon me in seconds.

"I'm going to enjoy devouring you," the wolfman said, pulling himself up my body. His claws dug into my flesh as he made his ascent.

"Damnit!"

The wolfman swiped at my throat. I raised my hand to block. A strange pulling sensation attacked my nails. I caught the wolfman's throat in my hand. A putrid scent filled the air. The wolfman fell on top of me, his throat gurgling. I pushed the man's twitching body off me and attempted to rise. The two others stopped and stared at me, their gaze focused on my hands. My nails had grown into sharp bird-like talons.

"Well, that's new," I said, flicking my nails. Blood splattered to the ground. One of the werewolves growled and charged with impressive speed. I twisted my body and swung my hand in an arch. I sidestepped, avoiding the werewolf, and it crashed into the bed in a bloody mess. The sole surviving werewolf turned on its heels and bolted out the door, whimpering as it ran away.

I hurriedly searched for my discarded gun and found it on the floor near the bed. A soft groan called out from above. I approached and came face to face with a naked man collapsed on the mattress. Grabbing a handful of hair, I yanked his head up. He released a gruff cry. I pointed my 9mm at his head.

"Listen up fleabag. Why are you after the girl?"

"Fuck … you …," the man said, smiling. What should have been pearly whites were tinted yellow.

I nodded. "Okay. Alright, fuck me."

I fired a round into his leg. The wolfman yowled, his body bucking. I resumed putting the gun to his head and flashed my own pearly whites at him. "Now, I'm gonna ask one more time. Why are you after the girl?"

When he didn't speak, I removed the gun from his head and aimed it at his knee cap.

The wolfman's eyes followed my sights and he stiffened. "Alright, alright. I'll talk."

"Spill it."

"A bounty. Some big shot placed a million-dollar bounty on her head. They want her alive."

"Who wants her?" I jammed the gun farther into his skull.

"I don't know. I just took the job. I don't know who posted it. I swear."

I released the man's hair and his head slammed down into the mattress. I shouldered my bag and exited the room, pulling the door shut behind me. I needed to find Harper. It would only be a matter of time before other bounty hunters caught up with her.

I began my search outside of the hotel. I checked the bushes and behind parked cars but she was nowhere to be seen. I took a few steps and my foot stepped into a puddle. That's when the scent hit me. A grotesque smell of rotten eggs. I pulled my foot out of the puddle. Red greeted me.

Werewolf blood.

I couldn't believe I was going to do this. I dipped my fingers into the blood and brought the scent up to my nose. I nearly gagged but forced myself to take in a deep breath.

"Damn," I said, brushing the blood onto my pants.

Harper's sweet scent was present. Chances were a werewolf had gotten a hold of her. I followed the blood trail. Someone had been hit pretty badly and was bleeding out. Due to the scent, I rationalized it was probably the werewolf. I followed the trail of blood across the street and stopped.

A broken-down theme park.

It was nothing too showy, just a small attraction in an equally small town. I approached the gate and stooped to my knees, looking for traces of blood. I spotted some on the inside of the fence. Taking a few steps back, I ran to jump the fence and made it successfully over to the other side.

I needed to hurry. Sure, Harper had managed to injure the werewolf but it was only a matter of time before other Shifters or Werewolves would show up. I continued following the blood until I came across a food concession stand. My nose twitched and I slammed my hand against it, blocking out that terrible scent.

I was close.

The scent led me about twenty feet away to a bumper car ride. Harper was next to one of the cars as the injured werewolf slinked toward her. Her gun was trained on the wolf.

"Don't make me do this," she said, pulling back the hammer.

I pulled out my own gun and fired. Blood and brain matter splattered onto the track. Harper shrieked, falling back into the car. She sat up quickly and I ran up to her, offering my hand.

"You okay?" I asked.

"Peachy," she said, dusting the cobwebs off.

"We should get back to the car before anything else shows up."

Harper nodded, following me back to the car. Once inside I locked the doors and drove away, leaving the death hotel behind us.

"Listen, I'm willing to help you but you have got to be honest with me. Why are these monsters after you?"

Anger flashed across Harper's face. "That's none of your business, Si."

"Harper. I literally just got bit multiple times by a werewolf while protecting you. It is my business."

Harper sat silently in the seat, not daring to look me in the eyes.

"Fine. Don't tell me, then our road trip ends here," I said.

I pulled the car over, hazard lights flashing. I had no intention of letting her leave, but she didn't need to know that. I looked at her for a long moment. Fear was etched into her features.

"If I tell you, you promise you won't leave me here?"

I nodded.

"Dru and our clan were researching the Alpha Gene. As you know, Alphas have the ability to turn humans into monsters. We were studying the Alphas' innate ability to control their kin, ones they have turned."

"What do you mean?" I asked, fearing the worse.

"They managed to replicate the Alpha's control. Now any monster, Alpha or not, can have an army of subservient followers."

"You mean to tell me that any monster could build an army if they wanted to? Why would Dru even ..." I said, anger tearing through me.

"We were under constant attack. We lost our Alpha about two weeks prior to my arrival with the Beauregard clan. We were sitting ducks. Dru figured having our own army would be the solution. What should we have done?"

"Not fuck with that," I said.

Harper reached into her bag, pulling out a junk drive. "The information is on this flash drive."

"Where did you get that?"

"I picked it up back at Beauregard Manor. It was in the box with the camera. Dru hid it there so it wouldn't stand out to intruders."

Mother must've wanted the information on the zip drive to amplify her Alpha powers. She would control every human on the planet if she had her way. She'd be unstoppable. I needed to trash the junk drive, better no one knew the secrets to the Alpha Gene. I could always bring Harper to Mother still securing my freedom. For all she would know the junk drive was lost during our little road trip.

"Give me the drive," I said.

Harper clutched the flash drive close to her chest. "No way."

"Harper if this gets into the wrong hands, it could lead to the extinction of the human race."

"I'm not giving over Dru's legacy," Harper said, desperation in her voice.

"You can't even protect it! Leave it with me. I can keep the information secure or destroy it if we have to."

"I can't destroy it."

"Harper you aren't thinking clearly."

"I'm thinking just fine," she said, anger laced through her voice.

"Give me the drive. I promise to keep it safe. You know I can better protect it."

Harper looked at me, eyes calculating. "Fine, but you have to promise me once we get to the safe house that you'll give it back."

"I promise Harper."

She held out the zip drive. I grabbed for it but she held on tight.

"Don't make me regret this," she said, releasing her grip on the drive.

***

The day's journey went off without any trouble. Harper mostly kept to herself, listening to music through her headphones. We spent most of the day weaving in and out of traffic, making the occasional bathroom stop, and just driving. We would make it to Sable by the next morning. Hard work, persistence, and the ability to make the mind-numbing drive really do pay off.

Though the closer we got to Sable, the more my heart betrayed me. I wanted to be able to focus on the mission but the more I looked at Harper, the more the guilt ate away at me. Harper was a pretty cool girl. She was kind, caring, sweet, and resilient. She was unapologetic for who she was, and I loved that about her. *Wait, did I just think "love"? No. I like that about her.*

I took a quick breath and glanced over at Harper. She was nodding off. I couldn't help but smile; she looked so peaceful and beautiful. I turned my attention back to the road and slammed on the brakes, nearly crashing into the car in front of me. Harper ripped off her headphones, looking around wildly.

"What happened?" she asked.

"Unexpected stop," I said apologetically.

She nodded and looked out the window. I followed her eyes and groaned. Traffic. Before us were two long lines of cars, all unmoving. I sighed once more, putting the car in park. Beside me Harper's breathing quickened. I looked over. Her eyes were shifting back and forth to each car around us.

"You okay?" I asked.

"I … I guess I'm just paranoid. It's just, I don't know … I mean any of these cars could be housing monsters. All our enemies over the last few days … I just want to get out of here."

I'd seen Harper scared over the last two days and I guess that everything was catching up with her. The poor girl, my heart went out to her. I wanted to protect her. To pull her in close and tell her everything was going to be okay, but I was the one bringing her to her possible death. I would just be lying to her, but perhaps I could at least make her last days free of pain and fear.

"Okay. Let's get out of here."

I pulled off to the right onto the side of the road and carefully maneuvered the car past others, until I reached the next exit some hundred fifty feet away. I pulled off the highway and glanced over at Harper, who had calmed down enough to lean back in her seat.

"How about we grab something to eat," I said, pulling into a burger joint.

"That sounds good."

I parked the car and we both exited. Harper stuck close to my side, looping her arm around mine. My heart raced in my chest. *Why is my heart racing?* We approached the counter, ordered bacon cheeseburgers, fries, and drinks. We found a table and Harper took a seat across from me.

"Will you be okay if I go wash my hands?" I asked.

"I don't think the monsters would attack in the open, like this," she said.

"If they did, BPMI would be all over them in seconds. I'll be right back."

I got up and went to the restroom, it was dingy and held an unpleasant scent. I quickly washed my hands and using paper towels opened the door. That's when I caught an unexpected sight. Two men, both close to my stature and age sat nestled around Harper. One, a blond, had his arm wrapped over her shoulders. The other, a box dye nightmare, had his hand on her lap.

"Get your hands off me," Harper said.

"Nah babe. Don't you want to come over to my place and have a little fun?" The blond said, moving his hand down to her breast.

"Hands off!" I said approaching the table as anger tore through me. Box dye lifted his hand immediately, backing off, but Blondie stayed in place. It looked like I would have to teach him a lesson, but Harper beat me to it. While the blond was distracted, she wound her arm back and sent a fist square in his nose. He fell out of his chair and collapsed to the floor. Blood flooded down his front. He stood up quickly, grabbing his nose.

"Man, fuck this," he said, running away.

I stared at Harper in awe. *Damn, what a woman.*

"You alright?" I asked.

"Just a couple of boys who wouldn't take no for an answer. I think I handled it."

"Hell yeah you did. Damn babe," I said.

Harper stared at me for a long moment.

Heat rose to my cheeks and I cleared my throat.

"Um … did you just call me …" Harper began to ask.

"It was nothing. Really, we should get our food and leave. Don't want to draw any more attention to ourselves."

Harper stood up and placed a light kiss on my cheek. "You're right. Let's go."

Intense heat burned from where Harper's lips had touched my skin. My mouth hung open, lips slightly parted. In that moment, I just wanted to grab her and kiss her, feel her, taste her. I pushed the thought away and followed after her as she grabbed our food from the counter.

Harper walked out the door. I followed, my feet feeling heavy and my mind fuzzy. Damn, she really was an amazing woman.

CHAPTER 9

SILAS

We drove in silence. Harper sat staring out the window while my thoughts raced. I couldn't stop thinking about that kiss; though it had just been on the cheek it was enough to drive me crazy. The way her lips felt against my skin. Her scent still hung heavy in my nose. I pushed down my primal instincts and drove the car, deciding to focus on the road instead.

Things were going well until her hand found its way onto my lap. I nearly swerved the car into the other lane from the shock. A car honked and the man driving it yelled a couple choice words as I went back into our lane. My eyes traveled down to Harper's delicate hand still resting in my lap. I took a quick breath, lightly picking it up and placed it in her lap. My heart beat loudly in my chest.

I glanced at Harper from the corner of my eye, and I could see a small frown forming on her lips. I turned back to the road and took a small breath.

***

We arrived in Sable, Pennsylvania at around 4 a.m., Mother's hunting ground. To say Sable was a large city was an understatement, it was ginormous. An unhealthy smog hung over the city. Large buildings kissed the sky and cars as numerous as an ant army flooded the streets. It would be another half hour or so until we reached Mother. At that point, my conscience was going crazy. The fever for Harper had only grown worse and now the thought of betraying her was killing me. One part of me screamed to tell her, to turn the car around and take her to safety, but another part wanted my freedom. No more house calls. No more Anya, Lazarus, Luther, or Mother. It would be a dream come true.

I looked over at Harper who was fast asleep. Did I really have it in me to turn her over? The time I had spent with her was short, but she had really made an indent on my heart. I had spent so much time alone over the last ten years, could I do it again?

Could I live without Harper?

I pulled out my phone from my pocket and flipped through the contacts, then dialed a number. The phone rang three times before a female voice answered.

"Silas?" Violet asked, her voice doused in sleep.

"Violet, I need your help."

"Silas," Violet said, her voice clearer, less sleepy. "What—God it's been nine years."

"I know, but I need your help. I'm back in Sable."

"What do you need?"

"Sanctuary," I said. "For me and my friend. Think you can work something out with Martin?"

"I don't know Silas, you made him pretty mad when you left here last time."

"Please Violet, I wouldn't be calling if it wasn't an emergency."

"Okay, I'll see what I can do. When will you be here?"

"I'm outside," I said.

"Jesus."

The line clicked dead.

Tudor Manor was located on the outskirts of Sable on the North Side. The building held an air of elegance and was made entirely out of white marble with big white columns. I parked the car in front of the steps and shook Harper awake lightly. She woke up immediately and gasped, her eyes landing on the manor.

"I've never seen a place so big or beautiful in my entire life," she said, stepping out of the car. "Is Dru inside?"

I took a quick breath. Harper was going to hate me. Would she stop talking to me or would she just get in the car and leave? I had already made my decision to tell her the truth but I didn't want to deal with the repercussions. A part of me wanted to die in that instant, to wither away into nothingness. I cared for Harper, deeply and I didn't want her to hate me, but she deserved the truth.

"Harper, I—"

Behind us the large black door was thrown open and out came Violet. She hadn't aged a day since the last time I had seen her. She wore a long purple dress that highlighted every curve on her body. She ran a pale hand though her long straight black hair. She went for Harper immediately, stopping about a foot away. She glared at Harper, her almond eyes turning into thin slits. The two stared at each other for a long moment before Violet turned toward me and smiled.

"I must say," Violet said, walking over to me and grabbing my arm in a tight hold, "it is so nice to see you again." She pressed her breast into my arm. They felt soft against me and I couldn't help but feel the heat rise to my cheeks. I glanced at Harper who only stared.

"Vi—"

"Come on," she said, cutting off my protest.

Violet led us through the large door and into the manor's foyer. Tudor Manor would walk circles around Ravnos Manor when it came to class and elegance. A large winding staircase sat off to the left with two leather armchairs resting underneath. A dark oak table sat in the foyer's center with a Grecian statue of a naked woman balanced on top. Violet dragged me a few more steps forward, my feet squeaking on the newly polished wood floors. Harper followed us inside, a vivid frown on her face. Her eyes never left me.

I pulled my arm free of Violet's grasp and walked over to Harper. She cast her eyes down. At that moment, I wanted to lift her up into my arms and kiss her. Convince her that Violet meant nothing to me. Defend myself from the hurt in her eyes. *Wait, why would there be hurt in her eyes. She doesn't like me, does she?*

"Vi. Do you have a room for us? We've had a long trip and just need to rest," I said.

"Yes. Of course, I'll have separate rooms prepared."

"No," Harper said quickly, "I'd rather stay with Silas. I don't sleep well by myself in new places."

"Right," Violet said, giving Harper a quick scan. "Follow me."

Violet led us down a long corridor, passing several doors. My mind began to drift, curious as to what lay past those doors. Suddenly, I was brought back to reality by Harper taking my hand.

"Sorry," she said, "it's hard to keep up. You all walk so fast."

I slowed down and matched Harper's pace, but she continued to hold my hand. I didn't fight it either. Finally, after several minutes of walking Violet stopped at a black door. It appeared to be just like any other door, no name plate or number to identify it. She opened it and gestured for us to enter. I stepped across the threshold with Harper still holding on to my hand.

The room was large and spacious. A beautiful oak dresser sat off to the right with a leather armchair accompanying it. The walls were dusted light gray and beautifully painted art pieces clung to them. A king size bed with a canopy was on the other side of the room. My heart did a flop as I realized what was happening. There was only one bed. I would have to share a bed with Harper.

My primal instincts told me that was fine, but I was a modern man, not an animal. I pushed the feelings down. *No. I need to tell her the truth. I doubt she'll want to have me after that anyway.*

"I trust that this room is to your liking?" Vi asked.

"It's great," I said.

"Then I'll take my leave," she said, closing the door behind her.

Harper released my hand and padded over to the bed, laying down. She pulled the covers up around her. I hesitated, remaining fixed in place. She flipped around on the bed, facing me, and looked at me with curious eyes.

"You coming?"

"I—I have something to tell you."

"I don't want to hear it. Please just come lay down with me. I just want to sleep."

"Harper—"

"Please Si."

I released a sigh and slipped off my shoes. I walked over to the bed, crawling in on the other side. A small smile graced Harper's lips and she rolled over, her back facing me.

"Come over here."

I followed her instructions, inching closer to her. She leaned back, her head now resting on my chest lightly. I sat still, too afraid she would feel my rapidly increasing heartbeat. Harper took my hand and pulled my arm around her shoulders. We lay like that for some time. I couldn't think through our embrace and for once I felt at peace. I could hear Harper's heart beating in her chest. Soft and slow. I focused on it, letting the continuous beat soothe me. I felt my eyes flash red. I turned my head away and Harper turned around to stare into them. She smoothed down my hair and brought her face close to mine. I stared into her honey brown eyes as her hand grabbed on to my forearm. Heat flowed through me. My heart beat increased. Her beauty entranced me. I leaned forward, going in for a kiss.

Our lips locked and my heart nearly exploded out of my chest. Her taste was sweet and I pulled her in closer to me. We stayed like that for some time, kissing, enveloping each other, before Harper pulled away, her heat leaving me wanting more. She smiled at me before rolling over once more, cuddling into me.

Harper's back brushed against my chest. My breath caught in my throat. She continued moving further back until her body was perfectly aligned with mine. Her curvaceous ass rested against my hip, and it took it all out of me not to pull her in closer.

Jesus. Calm down.

My mind was racing. I had intended to betray her and now I was betraying Mother. My mother would stop at nothing to get Harper, I knew that much. Would we be on the run forever? Or would it only be a short ride? Then there was the issue of Harper hating me once I told her the truth. She'd never trust me and might altogether abandon me.

Harper rolled over half doused with sleep and rested her head on my chest. I forced myself to take in air and watched as her head bobbed lightly. I was trying to be a gentleman but this girl was not making it easy. I guess letting her sleep on my chest wasn't a horrible thing. *It isn't taking advantage of her, is it?*

I allowed her to rest on my chest and soon her rhythmic breathing put me at ease and I fell asleep.

CHAPTER 10

HARPER

I awoke to Silas' soft breathing. My head lay cradled on his chest and it felt … nice. I didn't want to leave that position. I wanted to be close to Silas, enjoy the moment forever, and I knew it would piss off Violet. Ever since when we arrived last night, she had been giving me the stink eye and purposefully draping herself all over Silas. I felt a growl rising in my throat. I pushed it down at the sound of a light snore escaping Silas' lips. God, he was handsome. Muscular, lean, and strong, not to mention his protective personality had me on the brink. I wanted to disrobe him right there and demand he do things to me that would make a nun blush.

I instead went with cuddling, my back to his side. He rolled over in his sleep, his arm falling over my waist. He pulled me in closer. He held me like that for some time and I welcomed it.

A knock on the door ended our little spooning party. Silas awoke and, noticing the position we were in, nearly fell out of the bed. Man he may be hot, but he was not smooth. In that moment he was bundle of nerves fighting off the sexual tension that I know we both felt.

Silas got up quickly and opened the door. That annoying woman, Violet, was there to greet him. She frowned at me and when she looked at Silas, she practically threw herself at him. Silas caught the woman but quickly distanced himself by taking a step back once he knew she wasn't going to fall.

"Martin wishes to see you."

We quickly slipped into some more presentable clothes and followed Violet. She led us to a large dining hall with an equally large table meant to serve the whole clan, though only one man sat at the table. Martin, I presumed, was a handsome man. He was larger than Silas in both weight and height. He wore a flashy blue suit which I could only imagine cost a pretty penny. His brownish black hair was combed over to one side. He ran a tan hand over his lips and mustache as he finished what I figured was blood in his glass. One of his eyes was brown, the other was a milky white.

"Ah, Silas. I heard you had made your return. Good to have you back."

Silas stared down the man but didn't say anything.

"Thank you for having us," I piped up, hoping to cut down the tension in the room.

"And you must be Silas' new girl. Violet told me about you."

I smiled, bowing my head. Martin snapped his fingers and a woman dressed in all black scurried in to refill his glass.

"Perhaps I could interest you in a fine wine. Something to celebrate your return," Martin said, his fingers poised to snap.

"We need protection. Nothing more," Silas said in annoyance.

"Ah, you wouldn't happen to be on the run from your mother?" Martin asked.

I looked on in confusion. Protection from his mother? Wasn't she how he knew Dru? Why would she be trying to hurt us? I watched on in silence, hoping that something would start to make sense.

"Your silence is a resounding 'yes,'" Martin said, leaning his head on his fist. "Now as you know my protection isn't without cost. What will you trade me this time? Perhaps that beautiful woman you brought with you. I could always use a new wife."

I glanced over at Violet, her face radiating anger but she didn't fight Martin. I then looked to Silas, anger also clearly written on his face as his hands balled into fists.

"Back off Martin. Harper stays with me."

"Harper is it?" Martin sniffed the air, taking in my scent.

Silas slammed his fist on the table. "No games."

Martin smiled. "I only play to win." One second Martin was sitting in his chair, the next he was in front of a stunned Silas. Martin launched a fist, hitting Silas square in the nose. He stumbled backwards, blood gushing onto the floor. Martin sniffed the air and licked his lips. "Dhampir blood, now that will be a nice treat."

Silas regained his composure and held up his fists. I stepped in between them with my arms held out. Silas lowered his fist slightly.

"Move Harper," Silas said.

"Come on Silas you don't want to do this," I said, looking back and forth between him and Martin.

"Oh he does," Martin said.

"Harper *move*," Silas said once more.

I stood my ground. "You're better than this. Let's just leave. Please Si."

Silas lowered his fist. In Silas' moment of hesitation, Martin phased covering the distance between the two of them. Without warning Silas released a choked sigh, dropping to his knees. I dropped to his side, grabbing his shoulders and steadying him.

"My blood," Silas screamed, "it feels like it's on fire!"

Silas held up his hands and his veins protruded as liquid visibly flowed through them at an alarming rate. His eyes rolled up in his head showing only white. His mouth hung open in a permanent scream though no sound came out. He fell to the ground, lying motionless as sweat coated his face.

"What the hell did you do to him?" I demanded.

"A little plant called vervain—deadly to a Vampire. See Silas belongs to me, he traded his freedom nine years ago for protection from his mother, but that sneaky son of a bitch left leaving me with this," Martin said pointing to his milky white eye. "So I needed to teach him a lesson."

Martin put a syringe on the table. He snapped his fingers once more and two men appeared, hefting Silas off the ground. I hesitated in a moment of shock. He had hurt Silas. Anger ran through me. I wanted to tear him limb from limb. *How dare he hurt Silas.*

"Let Silas go, we're leaving," I said, rising and taking a step forward.

"You aren't going anywhere, Nephilim."

I stared at him in surprise. "How did you know?"

"I've only met one of your type before, but your scent is unforgettable. It's hard to pinpoint and most can't tell the difference between Nephilim and human, but once you know, you know."

He snapped his fingers again and Violet phased, appearing in front of me. Seconds later she grabbed me in a vice-like grip. I struggled against her but it was for naught.

"Take her to my chambers and have her prepared. Tonight she will conceive my child."

I stared at Martin for a long second. "If you think I'm having children with your dusty ass you have another thing coming!"

Violet pushed me forward, leading me out the dining hall and into a large room a few doors away. She shoved me to the ground in anger.

"Martin was supposed to be mine," she growled, "and you ruined everything."

"Look, I don't want your nasty—"

"Shut your mouth. Despite my personal feelings we must get you dressed. Martin will not tolerate insubordination," she said, grabbing at my shirt.

I batted her hand away in disgust. "If you think I'm going along with your little plan—"

"You will. Martin has a way of being very persuasive."

"So do I." I closed my eyes for a moment, gathering power into my palms. I knew using Heaven's Light would drain me of all my energy but what other choice did I have? My hands felt that familiar tingle and I pointed my hands at Violet. "I suggest you let me go right now or I'll toast you."

Violet stared at me for a long moment, before sighing and stepping aside allowing me to exit. "Hmm … looks like my hands are tied," she said in a sing-songy voice. "If you want to save Silas, you are going to need my help. I need help as well to dispatch Martin. Looks like we could strike up a deal."

I stared at Violet for a long moment. "You want my help to get rid of Martin? I thought you loved him."

"Love that disgusting prick?" She laughed. "I just used him and his love for me to rise through the ranks. Become his queen, gain power, but I'm tired of playing housewife."

I took a quick breath, "Okay, you've got a deal, but only because I need your help. Where is Silas?"

"He is on the ground floor in the holding cells." She threw me a white slip dress that revealed too much skin for my taste. "Put this on, I can lead you down there and get you past all the guards."

"You sure you want to trust me? I literally just threatened to turn you into a burnt marshmallow."

"As much as I'd rather have someone else's help, I know you're the best I got right now."

I began slipping off my clothes. "How do you know Silas?"

"I was engaged to Silas once," she said, walking over to a drawer and pulling out knives, "that is until I fell sick. I was a fangbanger. I used my body and blood to chase a high and soon I had too much exposure to Vampire venom, so I did the only thing I could think of. I pleaded with Martin to save my life. He did. He turned me and in the process I lost Silas. Silas said I had become a monster. I never stopped loving him and I can't bear to watch him spend his days as a comatose prize for Martin." Violet reached down, stashing the blades under her dress.

"Violet I—"

"Don't. It's obvious he's moved on. Now come on, we have to go save your boyfriend."

"He isn't my boyfriend."

But I sure do like the sound of it.

Violet led me down the long corridors and soon I became lost. I just hoped she wasn't tricking me. Soon, after walking for several minutes, we came across an elevator manned by two burly men. They refused to move.

"She's with me. Martin's orders. He wishes to procreate while forcing the Dhampir to watch."

The two men looked at each other with what could only be described as disgust and stepped aside, allowing us through. We rode the elevator down in silence. Finally, the button for the basement lit up and Violet took a deep breath. She drew two of her knives and held them at her side, ready to throw. The elevator door opened and five of Martin's strongest men greeted us with Martin at the forefront.

"Harper, I figured, but Violet, not you too. You were so devoted, a mindless follower," he said with a frown on his lips. "No matter, it seems you both need to be taught a lesson."

"I'll go for Martin, you have his men," Violet said, rushing forward.

"Great," I said, turning to the small battalion.

I sucked in a quick breath, brought forth Heaven's Light and aimed my palms at the middle of the charging fleet. Blinding light burst from my palms, roasting two of his men. Their skin cracked, turning black and the men faded away into dust. My eyes widened in confusion. I was never able to hone that much power before. I glanced down at the bracelet my mother had given me. Damn, that thing worked.

One of Martin's men phased in front of me grabbing me by the neck. I forced down the panic as my air supply dwindled. I closed my eyes and grabbed on to the arm holding my neck. I cast Heaven's Light. The vampire screamed as his hand turned to dust. I dropped to the floor, palms ready to fire. The last two of Martin's men turned around, booking it for the exit.

"Damn," I said in disbelief.

I scanned the room, looking for Silas. He sat against the far wall, unconscious and hands chained. I ran forward straight into a phased fist; the force of it toppled me backward onto the floor. Martin held Violet in a one-handed choke hold. I sat up, wiping blood from my lip.

I got up to my feet as Martin threw Violet at me. We landed in a heap tangled up in each other. Violet released a cough and forced herself to rise. I did the same, taking a deep breath. Violet phased, appearing behind Martin. As his back was turned, I charged him. Violet swiped a blade at Martin, and he leapt back straight into my extended my hand. My palm ran over his face, and I released Heaven's Light. Martin's shrill scream filled the basement before he fell over dead, what used to be his face now a bloody pulp.

Violet walked over, giving me a high five.

"Remind me to never get on your bad side ever again," she said.

I ran over to Silas, ignoring her. An IV drip had been set up beside him, pumping him full of vervain. I walked over to Martin's husk and began searching his pockets until I found a set of keys. Violet went to work disconnecting the drip while I undid his cuffs. Silas pitched forward, still unmoving. I searched for a pulse, placing my two fingers against his neck. A light beat fluttered against my fingertips. I released a shaky breath and swung one of his arms over my neck. Violet took his other arm and helped me heft him off the ground.

We walked for several minutes, half-dragging half-walking a discombobulated Silas through the corridors, until we finally reached the foyer. None of Martin's men fought against us; instead, they bowed as we walked past. It seemed that Violet had become the new leader. Violet opened the front door and eased Silas down onto the steps. I sat down beside him, allowing his head to rest in my lap. Violet left, disappearing in the foyer. I looked down at Silas, my heart going out to him. The vervain was heavy in his system, and he would most likely need blood to return back to normal.

Violet returned minutes later driving a green Ford Focus. She parked in front of us and got out the car to help me put Silas inside. Silas released a pained groan as sweat continued to profusely fall. Violet handed me a plastic bag filled to the brim with blood bags.

"Thank you," I said.

Violet took a deep breath then sighed. "I still love him you know, even though the bastard would rather have me die than become a monster. I will always love Silas. Take care of him."

I nodded. "What will you do now?"

"The Tudor Clan will rule under me and there will be some changes."

"Nothing too bad I hope."

Violet simply smiled.

I shook my head for a second and got into the car. The future of Sable and Tudor Manor were beyond my control. Right then I needed to focus on healing Silas. I got into the car without another word and drove away, leaving Tudor Manor behind.

CHAPTER 11

SILAS

The disgusting taste of blood coated my throat. I felt ravenous. I forced my eyes open only to find myself alone in a small motel room. I glanced around, eyeing the discolored wall and swore I saw a bug crawling across the windowsill. The bed was anything but comfortable and I didn't want to see what it looked like under a black light. I sat up slowly as pain wracked my body. Damn, that vervain really did a number on me.

Harper exited the bathroom and, upon seeing me awake, rushed over to my side. She placed her hand over my forehead and clicked her teeth. "You're burning up," she said, worry etched deep in her features. "Lay down and drink some blood."

She offered me a blood bag but I didn't take it. Instead, I sat back up and pulled Harper into a tight hug. She released a surprised gasp but soon hugged me back.

"What's this for?" she asked.

"I thought—I thought I was going to lose you to Martin. I had already lost Violet before to him. I just couldn't lose you too."

"I'm fine, really. Not even a scratch on me."

I smiled lightly, releasing my hold on her, and lay back down. "How long was I out for?"

"It's been three days," she said, not looking at me.

"Three days."

No wonder I was hungry. Three whole days lost in fever dreams. That's when the thought hit me. Mother. We needed to leave this area. It'd only be a matter of time before Mother found us. I forced myself to stand and Harper grabbed my arm, trying to pull me down.

"You need to rest."

"We aren't safe here."

She released my arm and crossed hers over her chest. "What the heck is going on? You've been acting weird ever since we got to the Tudor Manor. I know you are keeping something from me, just spill it."

"I—"

Suddenly, I felt a pang of pain go through me. I could hear Harper's pulse beating wildly in my ears. *Beat. Beat. Beat.* What was happening to me? I could never hear this well before. It felt as if my head was about to explode. I fell to my knees. Harper stared in shocked silence. *Beat. Beat. Beat.* I was going crazy. Raw, untamed hunger gnawed at me, threatening to spill over. I wanted blood. No, I *needed* it. *Need it. Need it. Need it.*

"Silas! What's wrong?"

Harper's pulse still beat loudly in my ears. *What if I just kill her now? Drink her blood. Let the metallic liquid run down my throat. End this hunger.* I forced the thought down, attempting to regain control.

My heart beat wildly in my chest. Harper brought her face to mine. In that moment I experienced things in such clarity. Her chest rising and falling. The perkiness of her breasts moving to her breathing. Her lips, slightly parted as she breathed. Her heart beat slow and light. Her blood rushed through her veins, and it took all my power to not lean down over her and syphon the blood from her neck. I pulled away.

Damn. How long will I be able to starve off this hunger?

I couldn't give in to the bloodlust. I was human, damnit. I always had been and it would stay that way. I'd already hurt Ximena and couldn't bear to do it to anyone else.

It felt as if the world was closing in. I needed fresh air. I attempted to turn away, but Harper grabbed my wrist. Another pang of immense pain ran through me. I felt my eyes flicker to red. I bowed over, clutching my stomach.

"Not now," I said.

All my mind could focus on was Harper. How sweet her blood would taste. A small laugh escaped my throat. I shook my hand free and exited the room quickly. I entered the bathroom, locking the door shut behind me.

I was a monster. Tears welled up in my eyes. I would always be plagued by an inhuman hunger that was never satisfied. I settled myself in front of the mirror. Red eyes stared back at me. I swallowed hard and slid down with my back against the door.

There was a knock. "Silas?"

I put my head in my hands. "Yeah."

"Are you alright?"

"Yeah."

"Open the door."

"I can't," I said. "I might hurt you."

"You won't hurt me. I know you won't."

Taking a deep breath, I stood up to unlock the door. "Harper ..." I began.

She opened the door and pulled me into a tight hug. She held on for some time before releasing me. Her gaze trailed to my hand. She took mine in hers and studied them together. "You're shaking."

"It's nothing," I said, pulling my hand away.

She offered her wrist to me. "You need blood. Take mine."

I shook my head, not looking at her.

She scratched at an old scab. A drop of blood pooled on her flesh. I caught the scent and couldn't help but look. Hunger gnawed at me. Saliva collected in my mouth. *Blood.* The life force to any human and here it was right in front me, tantalizing. My breath caught in my throat. God, I needed that blood. No, I wanted it. I wanted it so badly. To feel its cooling liquid go down my throat. Just one bite, that's all I needed. I would drain her dry. I felt my mouth open, and trickles of spit flowed down my chin. I was so close to having her, all for myself. I grabbed her forearm, feeling her pulse beat softly in my hands.

I couldn't pull away. My teeth grazed her wrist and she stiffened. I bit down on Harper's flesh, and she released a small squeal. I began to drink and her knees buckled. Her blood was sweet, unlike regular blood. I slurped it down as I held on to the girl, my hand supporting her back. Her eyes rolled up in her head revealing white. She moaned against me as my Vampire venom went into her skin.

I don't know how long I drank for, but soon things began to clear. My hunger diminished into nothingness. I released my fangs from Harper's flesh and she went limp. Fear raced through me. *Have I killed her?* Harper released another moan. My heart raced, relief flowing through me.

Vampire venom was meant to subdue a human's movements so that a vamp could feed without its prey escaping.

It was an evolutionary benefit that Vampires had developed. Along with the paralysis came a high, a sense of euphoria. Most humans who experienced the bite of a Vampire developed a dependency on the venom almost instantly. Harper was experiencing that high. It would only take about a half hour to come down from, but it was severely over-powering. I carried her to the bed, fighting off my worry for Mother, and laid her down gently. I pulled the covers up around her and allowed her to sleep.

Harper slept for about an hour. Then she sat up slowly, grasping her head. She groaned. Headache, a common symptom of the venom leaving the body. I came to Harper's side, offering her a cup of water. She took it gratefully and drank it down.

"Silas," she said, "I know you aren't telling me the whole truth."

I closed my eyes, my heart quickening. "You're right. I'm not."

She stared at me with sad eyes. I looked past them, taking a seat on the edge of the bed.

"Dru is dead and I was never sent by her to retrieve you."

Harper's eyes widened in shock. I couldn't dare meet them.

"You lied to me," she said breathlessly.

"I was sent to retrieve you and bring you to my mother in exchange for my freedom. Harper you have to under-stand, my mother—what she did to me—she's the one who awakened my vampiric side. Forced me to kill an innocent woman. I knew if I stayed with her—"

"So you thought it best to betray me. How could I have been so stupid?"

"That was my plan at first, but—I—I couldn't. Not after I got to know you. Harper, you are an amazing woman. I can't hurt you."

"You already have."

"Harper." I reached out my hand.

"Don't touch me!" She shook her head rising from the bed. She stumbled, walking to the motel door. "Don't ever talk to me again!"

She threw the door open and gasped. Standing before her were the Twins. Lazarus reached a hand out, grabbing Harper and knocking her out cold.

"Mother wants you home," Lazarus said.

"Come home brother," Luther said, reaching for me.

***

I was being dragged through the abandoned back streets, my useless body sliding against the asphalt. Luther had me by the collar, like a mother dog to her puppy, but there was no love there. I could barely breathe but I'm sure Luther didn't mind that. Lazarus had disappeared with Harper somewhere during my struggle with Luther, damn bastard. Shit, I couldn't stop it. I tried to set things right with Harper, but I was too late. Harper was going to die because of me.

I fell to the ground, finally able to take in more air. I gasped like a fish out of water. Air burned as it made its way into my deprived lungs. Then, without warning, Luther screamed and blood spattered onto my face. I wiped the blood away and sat up. In front of me was an interesting scene.

Anya stood blocking our path in a deserted alleyway. She assumed a fighting stance, her blade drawn. Her purple hair was pulled back into a ponytail, something I had learned over the years that meant she was ready for a battle. My eyes trailed to her blade; its silver was coated in dark blood. Luther's hand was abandoned on the road in between my feet. Luther clasped at his stub, growling. I sat dumbfounded. What was Anya doing?

"There," she said, "now you and Lazarus are identical twins again. Missing hand and all."

"What are you doing?" Luther growled.

Anya ignored him. She looked at me and said, "You alright?"

I gave her a weak thumbs up.

She turned back to Luther and in the blink of an eye she vanished. Luther glanced around and then screamed again. Blood sprayed from his back. Anya appeared a second later behind him. He roared with rage, his chest heaving. He flashed for a second disappearing. Anya followed suit, leaving me sitting alone.

They appeared a second later some fifty feet away. More blood dripped down from Luther's leg. His body slid forward as his leg was severed from his body. Luther lay on his back and turned his confounded gaze at Anya.

"Why, Anya?" He asked in a pathetic voice.

Anya slammed her blade into Luther's head, silencing him. His body spasmed for a moment before going still. Anya disappeared, phasing in front of me. I stared up at her, unmoving. Shit, this was my end. I would end up just like Luther with a blade through the brain.

Instead, Anya knelt down and offered me her hand.

I stared at her for a minute, unable to think.

"What?" I said bewildered.

"Can you stand?"

"Uh … why? Aren't you going to kill me?"

Anya grasped my hand and hefted me to my feet. "We need to go. It'll only be a matter of time before the authorities arrive."

She vanished then appeared before a parked car. I followed suit running, but something felt different. I felt the wind bash around me and for a second I thought I had been swallowed up by a tornado. Anya stared at me in confusion.

"You phased," she remarked. Moving past the confusion she then said, "Get in the car."

I followed her instruction and she sped off, tires squealing behind us.

"Anya," I said.

"I simply despise that name," Anya said. "It's Mother's pet name for me. Call me Anastasia."

"Anastasia … What the hell is going on? You saved my life. Why?" I asked, dumbfounded.

"Don't think I'm doing it for you. I did it because I need allies," Anastasia said curtly.

"Allies? For what?" I questioned.

"To overthrow Mother," she said simply.

"Overthrow her?"

"Yes. Mother has killed Lord Ravnos and converted all his followers."

I let the words sink into my tired brain. It was happening. "Where's Harper?"

"Mother has taken her," Anastasia answered.

I slammed my fist against the car's interior.

"Calm down little brother. I have eyes on her, but we need to hurry."

"Dammit. We need to save Harper. I can't abandon her."

"Yeah no kidding, Harper is a Nephilim."

I let the words sink in. Harper was a Nephilim. She wasn't human, not fully anyway. That whole time I had thought Mother wanted Harper for her knowledge, but she actually wanted Harper's powers. Powers that would destroy the whole world and leave humankind bowing at Mother's feet—and

I had given my mother that power. Hand-delivered it. Guilt gnawed through me.

"Hey," Anastasia said, drawing me from my thoughts. "We need to get Harper separated from Mother. With her blood, Mother will gain the power of mind control. She will be able to control anyone she pleases. She already has support from many clans. We cannot let that happen."

I nodded. After all my years of hunting I had never come across a Nephilim, but I had heard rumors, fairytales really, of the power of their blood. If used correctly they could control entire masses. Of course, these were just stories that monsters told their little ones to help them go to bed blood thirsty for revenge and control of the human race. Somehow Mother had done it: took what was a fairytale and made it real.

I had done this, played the biggest hand in the destruction of humankind. I needed to fix this.

Anastasia glanced at me, reached into the glove compartment, and pulled out a gun. She passed it to me and I weighed it in my hand. Mother was going to pay. I was going to see to that personally.

CHAPTER 12

SILAS

Willingly going back to the Ravnos Manor was something I'd never thought I'd do in a million years, but there I was at its front door. The smell of blood hit me before I even entered the room. The foyer was in disarray. Beyond it, chairs were strewn about and toppled over. The gray walls were decorated in blood. Sitting on a chair a mere few feet away was the body of the now-deceased clan leader, Lord Ravnos. I never imagined I'd see the Alpha dead. I had only laid eyes upon him once back when I lived in Ravnos Manor. He was truly a powerful Alpha. He had turned many humans into vampires—not an ordinary task for the average monster. His corpse had pale blond hair and even paler skin, with high cheekbones that would make any runway model jealous. And his eyes, blood red. He was a strange looking Vampire, but again, powerful. And Mother had dispatched him like he was nothing more than trash. Anastasia walked up to the corpse and studied it. Cuts and burns were carved deep into the flesh and on some parts the bone. His head hung on to his body by one thin cord of flesh.

I resisted the urge to gag.

Then I tensed as I felt a collection of gazes on us. My hand instinctively reached for my gun. A woman stepped out from the shadows. She had shoulder-length black hair that curled at the ends. Her skin was a light tan and on her forehead was the Hindu Jain Bindi. She wore tactical gear and in a one-handed grip she carried a sawed-off shotgun. She put her fist to her chest and Anastasia did the same in greeting.

"Report, Hema. What has my mother been up to?"

"As you can see, Lenora has already dispatched Lord Ravnos. She has the Beauregard girl."

"Her status on the mind control serum?" Anastasia said, walking forward.

More vampires dressed in tactical armor came from the shadows surrounding us. I resisted the urge to grab my gun and followed after the two women. The vamps followed as well.

"She hasn't managed to crack it yet but she has managed to get a cult following right under Lord Ravnos' nose. They took him out when he was at his weakest."

"The daytime?" I questioned.

"Yes, Dhampir," Hema said, annoyed.

"Address him as Silas. He is my brother and he fights against Mother for the same reasons we do."

"Yes of course, Lady Anastasia. My apologies, Lord Silas."

I stared at Hema for a long moment. *Lord*, I had never been called that before. Honestly it just didn't sit well. I clasped my hand to Hema's shoulder. "Just call me Silas," I said offering a smile.

She nodded back and continued debriefing Anastasia.

"We are waiting for your call, my lady. We need to attack Lenora when she is at her weakest and before she develops the serum."

"Daylight will be here in a matter of minutes. We will lay low until tomorrow night," Anastasia said.

"No way," I said, coming between the two women. "Harper is out there and I need to find her. I can go alone."

"Don't be stupid, brother."

"I can't just leave her."

"Harper will be safe until Mother creates the serum. We still have time. We cannot rush into this blindly," Anastasia said.

"Look, it's great that you have your own cult but the woman I care about is being held captive by the worst baddie out there."

"Silas, my men are watching closely, covertly. Mother requires a Nephilim's blood among other things to create the serum. Mother will pair the Nephilim's ability of mind manipulation with Alpha blood to create the ultimate mind control concoction. I understand you are worried for your friend, but Mother will not dispose of her, not for a long while. She'll need plenty of blood for the serum and she can't do that with a dead girl. Right now Harper is safe. We must wait a few hours or else all my planning will be for nothing. I know it'll be hard, but you must wait. If we mess this up, Harper won't be the only person who dies."

***

Waiting. *God how I hate waiting.* Sitting around while Harper could be being tortured or worse felt horrible. Though my body craved sleep I just couldn't bring myself to relax. Several hours had passed and I spent the day wearing a hole through the floor. *What unimaginable horror is Harper going through? Is she even still alive?* A knock rapped against the door, sending me out of my spiraling thoughts. I went to the door, hand holding my gun. Hema stood there, sawed-off shotgun still in hand.

Night had finally come.

I was loaded up into a vehicle with Hema at the wheel. She wore the same black tactical gear that she had worn the night before; guns were strapped all over her.

"Where's Anastasia?" I asked, buckling in.

"Your sister has already left; she is in the tunnels as we speak."

We rode on in silence for a few minutes before Hema spoke. "You ready for this?"

I nodded. My mother needed to pay for kidnapping Harper, for making my life hell. Her life of tyranny needed to end. I checked my gun to make sure everything was working smoothly.

"Open the glove compartment," Hema said.

I followed her orders and found only a wooden stake. I took it in my hands. To anyone that had heard the rumors spread by Vampires, most believed only a stake to the heart could kill a vamp, but that simply wasn't true. Bullets were just as effective if aimed at the brain or heart. Though there was some truth to the legend and a stake *could* kill a vampire, it was an incredibly slow process and less effective than a spray of bullets. But it was better to have a stake than no weapons at all.

"We're going old school here?"

"Take it, sometimes guns fail. This doesn't."

I pocketed the stake. "So why are you after my mother?"

"I have no real reason besides doing what is right. I am a dutiful follower of your sister. She is the leader that we need to bring us into peace. For too long Vampires have run in the shadows, hunting humans. Killing mercilessly. We believe that we can coexist with humans, regain what we once lost, our humanity."

"You think Anastasia can lead you into peace?"

"Your sister is rough around the edges but she is a woman of peace. All she does, she does for her people." Hema took another turn. "Even killing her own mother."

"Mother by now has to be one of the most powerful vamps on the east coast. It'll take more than a few of us to stop her," I said.

"We will try regardless," Hema assured me.

"Take a left up here. I have an idea," I said, pointing.

"What are you planning? It mustn't take long as we must meet up with Lady Anastasia."

"Won't take long, just picking up a friend."

***

Fuzzy had his head sticking out of the car window, tongue flapping in the wind. The little Werewolf was like a dog in traffic—no cares or concerns, just enjoying the smells. Though we hadn't maintained contact, Fuzzy had thanked me immensely when we picked him up from the monster rehab center. Said he was doing much better after being separated from his Alpha and had even started up a new life as a high school student. The little fuzzball said he owed everything to me, that if I hadn't spared him he would've died a monster, but now he was righting all his sins by volunteering and helping to mentor younger Werewolves.

Though the car ride was a nice one to Fuzzy standards, it wasn't a long one, sadly about ten minutes. We pulled to a stop at an alleyway. We all exited the car and entered the dark. It took a minute for my eyes to adjust but Fuzzy stuck close, half guiding me through the darkness. We came across a manhole. Hema knelt down and began prying the lid loose.

"Alright," Hema said once the manhole was open. "The other teams are already down there fighting. They've cleared a path for us. Once inside we will rendezvous with Lady Anastasia and then take out Lenora." She turned to face me. "The Beauregard girl is reported to be in a tunnel with Lenora but none of the men have been able to get close."

"Leave it to me," I said, tightening my grip on my gun.

Hema nodded, throwing me a headlamp. "Take this." With that, she jumped into the manhole.

I went next, followed by Fuzzy. The tunnels under Sable were dark. A vampire's playground. They mainly used the tunnels for getting rid of victims and clean up.

I flicked on the flashlight and began walking. The tunnels were quiet, even to my extra sensory hearing. I looked around as we made our way deeper into the underground. The walls were spaced out enough that a big rig could fit. There were no markings to show which direction you were heading. Everything was wet, condensation dripping off the walls.

Fuzzy still stuck close by, his breathing loud in my ears. His claws clicked against the pavement and due to the dripping ceiling he soon began to smell like wet dog. My attention was drawn away from the scent when I nearly tripped over a discarded hand. I gripped my gun tightly and switched off the safety.

Farther up the tunnels we came across more body parts, ones I assumed were a mixture of Mother's and Anastasia's men. Their bodies had been torn apart and it seemed I had my answer to whose hand I had tripped over. A serious battle had taken place down there. Unbeknownst to the human world, a war for the mind control serum was taking place right under their feet.

Hema walked past me with agile grace and approached two men who were hiding in the shadows.

"Report," Hema said.

"Lenora's entry-level guards have been dispatched. We have conquered this section of the tunnel."

"What of Lady Anastasia?"

"She is farther ahead. The last report stated she was squaring off against her brother Lazarus."

"And of the Beauregard girl?"

"No one has made contact. Lenora has taken her deep within the tunnels."

Hema nodded and walked past the two vamps. I followed behind, anxiety gnawing at my stomach. I needed to find Harper fast, I didn't want to imagine what horrors she had been subjected to. We walked for some time until we came across a section that divided into two entry points. Hema paused for a moment, unsure of which way to go.

"Silas you and the Werewolf take the left tunnel. I'll take the right."

"I can't let you go by yourself," I said.

"Listen, Dhampir. You need to stop worrying about me and find the Beauregard girl. I can take care of myself."

I stood conflicted for a moment. I did need to find Harper and fast but allowing Hema to go alone in a vamp-infested tunnel was suicide. Hema would be outnumbered. She must have known that.

Hema placed her hand on my shoulder and nodded. She made her way into the right tunnel, fading into the dark.

Getting over my conflicted feelings I led the way down the left tunnel, Fuzzy following close behind. The tunnel seemed to go on forever, twisting and turning down long corridors. Staying the course, we came across an open room. It was two stories tall with a balcony overlooking the hall. This was quite common in Vampire tunnels—typically used for gatherings. I looked at the balcony and saw Mother with a barely conscious Harper. I withdrew my gun and pointed it at Mother.

"So, you've turned against your own mother," Mother said in a low voice.

Footsteps approached behind me. Anastasia walked past me into the middle of the room, holding the head of Lazarus. She dropped it to the ground, and it tumbled away a few feet. A look of anger was etched in Mother's face. "Anya, you would betray me too?'"

Anastasia smiled, flicking her blade to the side, blood splattering to the ground. "I've lived in your shadow long enough," Anastasia said.

Mother laughed. Dark and wicked. Her laughter filled the whole hall. A shiver ran up my spine. Then the sound of running footsteps quickly filled the air. Entering the room were a collection of Shifters and Werewolves, bounty hunters, none loyal to Anastasia, but to the money on Harper's head. I cursed under my breath and turned to face them, gun flicking back and forth between all our opponents.

"This is a family affair," Mother said, "I don't appreciate the interruption."

"Give up the research Lenora!" one man shouted from the group of Shifters.

"Give it to us!" A man from the Werewolves said.

"Silence! You insolent freaks!" Mother shouted.

The ground began to shake underneath us. A wall directly under Mother began to slide open. From the shadows came a monstrous humanoid beast. It stood at nine feet tall with pale green skin. Large vine-like tendrils wrapped around its face and neck and slowly moved, flicking about. Its ears were long and pointed like antennas. One arm scraped against the ground as it took a step toward us. The other carried a large battle axe made up of wood and steel. It took another step, axe dragging on the floor. An audible whimper ran through the room. Some of the Shifters and Werewolves attempted to flee. Mother had already disappeared from above with Harper. The monster whipped its axe in an arch, taking out three of the fleeing monsters. Bodies were split in half and blood flew to the ground like rain. Anastasia stood her ground, raising her blade. Fuzzy whined and backed away slowly, ears pressed flat against his head.

"Shit," I said, breathlessly, "Mother has a fucking troll."

CHAPTER 13

SILAS

The troll wound back for another strike, axe scraping against the floor. I took off at a run, aiming my gun for the troll's knees. I fired two shots, and both found their target. They didn't even phase the beast. Anastasia charged the monster head on, her blade locked on its arm. Anastasia hit, but little damage was done. Picking up speed, the troll's axe came down to chop a werewolf clean in half. The troll raised his axe once more, his target now Fuzzy. Fuzzy didn't move, instead he tucked his tail between his legs and his eyes grew as large as saucers. I needed to move fast or Fuzzy would be mincemeat.

I charged after Fuzzy, putting my full speed into my run. I tackled into him, slamming my shoulder into his side just as the axe came down. I forced myself to do a tuck and roll, narrowly avoiding steel.

"Stay by my side!" I shouted at Fuzzy.

Fuzzy shook his head and positioned himself nearby, a low growl escaping his lips. The troll began to charge forward, his heavy battle axe releasing sparks against the concrete.

The troll, though large, took up amazing speed that could be matched by Anastasia's. It phased escaping my vision. How was that even possible? Trolls couldn't phase, they were usually slow and have clunky movements, but this troll was different. Seconds later the troll appeared lifting a hyena Shifter off the ground with its long arm. Its green tendrils whipped back and forth, slashing at the hyena. The Shifter struggled in the troll's embrace. The troll brought the Shifter to its mouth and chomped down, swallowing a piece of the Shifter's skull. Blood ran down the troll's front and it dropped the body to the ground.

The room grew quiet, all the monsters defeated in battle, leaving only Anastasia, Fuzzy, and I as last survivors. Anastasia phased, disappearing from view. The troll followed suit, leaving Fuzzy and me looking around like damn fools.

Suddenly the troll appeared in front of me, battle axe inches from my face. Anastasia stood behind me, her blade holding back the beast's mighty axe. Her arm quivered as she held off the troll's attack.

"Attack it now!" Anastasia shouted.

"Fuzzy go for its back!" I shouted.

Fuzzy ran around the monster disappearing from view. I fired my gun, three rounds straight at the troll's heart. Anastasia grabbed my collar and yanked me back, her blade withdrawing from the axe. The axe crashed down into the cement, becoming stuck.

I reloaded my gun with practiced speed and sent another four rounds into the troll's head. Surely that would kill him? The bullets bounced off the troll's dome. I stood dumbstruck for a moment. Fuzzy bit down on the monster's ankle, but the troll barely noticed. It simply kicked its leg out, sending Fuzzy flying. He crashed down in a heap some ten feet away. He attempted to stand but fell over, his whole body shaking.

Anastasia side-stepped from behind me and phased. A fraction of a second later, her blade connected with the troll's neck, slicing it with mastered precision. The beast blocked the attack with its arm. Something about that moment felt off. I replayed the attack in my mind. The troll never blocked any attacks, but the second Anastasia went for its neck, it went on the defensive.

I smiled. "Go for the neck! I think that is its weak point!"

I fired two more shots at the troll's throat. It phased away. I glanced around, trying to figure out its next attack. My heart sank. "Fuzzy! You have to get out of there now!"

Anastasia ran forward, disappearing. I looked to Fuzzy, waiting for the troll to appear but he never did. Instead, Anastasia's shout rang loudly through my eardrums.

"Silas!"

I was hefted off the ground in the troll's iron grip, its hand wrapped around my chest. My breath caught in my lungs and my gun clattered to the ground. I struggled in the troll's grip as his tendrils tugged at my legs. Anastasia charged, screaming. The beast caught her blade in its free palm. The troll lifted me up to its face and smiled. Its teeth were a dentist's worst nightmare. Black swam across my vision. Thinking quickly, I dropped my arms to my side and retrieved the wooden stake. In one swift motion, I stabbed the troll's neck with all my strength. The stake caught in flesh and I pulled down, causing a long gash. The troll yowled and dropped me. I crashed into the ground at its feet.

Air rushed into my lungs and, though my body pleaded with me not to move, I forced myself to crawl for my gun. I quickly reloaded and fired two more shots at the troll's exposed neck. My bullets hit and the troll rocked back from the impact.

Anastasia charged forward, using my back as a step and launched herself into the air. Her blade moved with trained precision, slicing the troll's throat.

The troll ducked, grabbing a nearby wolf corpse and lifting it over its mouth. The troll squeezed tightly allowing blood to drip in an overpowering wave. I resisted the urge to gag at the scent. The troll swallowed the blood and soon its neck began to stitch together as if it had taken no damage.

"What the hell? It can heal by blood," I said in disbelief.

In anger the troll phased and grabbed a distracted Anastasia around the waist.

"You small, insolent fools," the troll said. "Stop your fighting or I will crush the girl."

I stared in complete disbelief. The troll was talking. Trolls were not very bright and couldn't form sentences; they communicated, if one could call it that, in body language and grunts.

This was no normal troll.

Anastasia kicked her feet together, a knife appearing at the tip of her shoes. She kicked upwards, the blade landing in the troll's hand. It released her with a click of its teeth. Anastasia fell to the ground, then phased beside me.

"I will not be used as a bargaining chip," she said, wiping a piece of lilac hair out of her face.

The troll spoke, his voice deep, rumbling. "Pitiful humans wallowing in filth, don't you see we are doing what Lenora wants, when we should be attacking her together?"

"Why would you want to attack her?" I asked.

"She tore me away from my home. Experimented on me, tortured me. I want my revenge."

"How do we know that you are telling the truth? For all we know this could be a trap set by Mother," I said.

The troll released an agitated sigh. "I know Lenora's whereabouts. She spoke of them freely around me, thinking I was an insolent fool. I can lead you directly to her and the girl that you seek."

"You can take us to Harper?" I asked.

"Yes," the troll said simply.

"Lead the way," I said, pocketing my gun.

"Silas, no, we still don't know if we can trust him," Anastasia said, grabbing my arm.

"That doesn't matter right now, we need to save Harper. I'm going with him."

Anastasia crossed her arms in defeat. "Troll, if you are leading us astray, my blade will end you."

The troll smiled. "I guarantee you safe passage, for I need assistance killing that devil woman."

"Damn our mom is a bitch to everyone," I said under my breath.

The troll's body began to shift and contort, his skin turned a pale beige and his tendrils turned into what could only be described as dreadlocks. He bent over, his body shrinking. The troll, now human, stood at about seven feet tall.

"This should work enough as a disguise. For a name, call me Druze," the troll said.

Sudden exhaustion hit me and I fell on my ass, breathing hard. The sound of footsteps filled the room. Anastasia's men, led by Hema, joined us. Hema stopped in her tracks as she spotted the abnormally large human. She aimed her gun at him, but Anastasia stepped in front to block shot. Hema placed her fist against her chest greeting Anastasia.

"Report," Anastasia said.

"We have successfully thinned out Lenora's men," Hema said.

"Hema, you and the others stay here. Silas and I will take on our mother," Anastasia ordered.

"But Lady Anastasia, her men let it slip that she's already created the mind control serum—who knows how many are under her control," Hema begged.

"That's an order," Anastasia said, her voice growing cold.

Hema stiffened then nodded, a look of worry crossing her face.

"Guard Fuzzy," I said, standing up.

"Your friend will be safe with us," Hema said, placing her hand over her chest again. "Fight strong and do not die ..." Hema looked passed me to the seven-foot-tall man. "Who is the tall guy?"

"He's coming with us," I said simply.

Anastasia turned and walked through the gate that the troll had come out of. I followed close behind, gun drawn. We walked down the tunnel, my heart thundering through my chest.

"Silas, we need to discuss our plan of attack. Going in blind will lead to our certain deaths," Anastasia said.

"She is right Dhampir. Your mother will not be easy to defeat," Druze said, taking the lead.

"What did you have in mind?" I asked.

"When we find Mother, I will face her head on. I will act as a distraction while you deliver the killing blow," Anastasia said coldly.

"You think I can kill mother?" I asked in disbelief.

"You will have to," Anastasia said.

"Mother is faster, smarter, and stronger than me. I'd be lucky just to land one shot," I said.

"That's because you haven't been fighting at your full capacity. You've always held back. But now is not the time to do that," Anastasia replied.

Silence befell us in the tunnels. We continued on, the only sound our feet hitting the concrete. Then Anastasia spoke, her voice deafening compared to the silence we just endured. "There is something else I wanted to tell you. In case this is where I meet my end."

"Anastasia …"

"I'm sorry. I've wronged you Silas. So many times. I used to think I was doing the right thing, but I realized I was only covering my own ass. I didn't want to die and I feared Mother. If I could change things … been there for you more, I would. I honestly would," Anastasia said, her voice soft.

I paused stopping in my tracks.

"Thank you," I whispered.

We made it to the end of the tunnel, leading us into a large planetarium above ground. I glanced up at the revolving ceiling which was currently closed. Chairs lined the room and a large stage sat in its center. Mother stood on the stage with Harper balanced on a chair.

I looked to Harper and my heart sank. She was barely conscious, her head drooping. I approached the stage hurriedly. Anger surged through my flesh, warming me.

"What did you do to her?" I shouted.

"So, you've finally decided to join the party," Mother said, ignoring me.

"Give her to me now," I growled.

"Oh hush. Your little girlfriend is fine. Aren't you darling?" Mother grabbed Harper's face in her hands.

"I'll kill you." I trained my gun on my mother. She didn't even blink. Instead she phased, disappeared, and reappeared a second later, her face barely and inch from mine. She smiled, sending a punch with the force of a speeding train to my face. I dropped to the ground instantly. Anastasia charged but before she could land a strike Mother caught the blade in her hand. Blood flowed free and Mother tightened her grip on the blade. She pulled Anastasia toward her and sent a kick to her stomach.

Anastasia vomited blood and crashed to her knees. Druze phased in front of Mother, landing a punch to her face. Mother smiled as blood dripped down her nose. She wound her arm back with inhuman speed and punched Druze in his neck. He fell to the ground gasping for air.

Mother reached down and effortlessly picked me up by the collar. Pain screamed through my neck and face. I swung a weak fist at her, but she blocked it with her bleeding hand. She phased, carrying me along with her and dropped me at Harper's feet.

Harper stirred gently, her eyes fluttering open.

"Silas," she whispered.

I struggled to rise to my feet, but Mother slammed her high heeled foot down on my back, pushing me further into the ground.

"I'm so glad you could both join me for this momentous occasion," Mother said.

Harper's fingers twitched as she attempted to reach for me. I reached back for her, but Mother's heel dug deeper into my back. I groaned underneath her.

"Isn't this just cute. You actually had the audacity to betray me and for what? A girl?" Mother laughed.

Anastasia appeared before Mother, throwing a kick. Mother simply ducked, grabbed me by my shirt, and flung me at my sister. I crashed down on Anastasia hard, some feet away.

"And you, Anya, my only daughter. You've betrayed me too." Mother sighed. "You know I actually had a plan for you Anya. You were to rule beside me as my right-hand woman, but you squandered that. And for what?"

I pushed myself up on my hands, body badly shaking. Mother was strong. Stronger than any vamp I had ever faced.

"Peace," Anastasia spat.

"Peace?" Mother said in humor.

"It's something you could never hope to understand," Anastasia said, her voice icy and cold.

"Then you will die first, all in the name of peace!" Mother shouted.

Druze phased in front of Anastasia, grabbing a hold of our mother's arm.

"And why the hell do *you* keep interfering?" Mother spat.

"My name is Druze. Troll from the Litfield Mountains. You stole me from my home. Tortured me and experimented on me."

A small smile graced her lips. "I see. So, our experiments gifted you with intelligence. Isn't that just cute."

"That's not all," Druze said, throwing a fast punch I could barely track at Mother's face.

With Druze's grip on her arm loosened, Mother pulled herself free and ripped Druze's arm off with her. She flung the appendage to the ground as Druze released a low cry. Mother phased back in front of me. Just as she was about to strike, Anastasia phased to block Mother's attack with her own body. Blood trickled down Anastasia's chin. Mother's six-inch claws were dug into Anastasia's stomach. My sister's breathing became haggard as mother twisted her claws, drawing more blood. Mother released her grip on Anastasia and she fell to the floor, blood pooling around her.

"Anastasia!" I shouted.

"Oh yes, my last son," Mother said, stalking toward me. "My most treasured."

I attempted to crawl away but Mother grabbed me by my hair, forcing my head up. Pain seared through my scalp.

"I'm willing to forgive you Silas. All you need to do is kill the girl, regain my trust."

I moved my lips, my words barely audible. Mother pulled me closer to her face.

"Come again?" Mother asked.

"Fuck … you …" I spat.

Mother threw me to the ground, sending a kick into my back. "You ignorant boy. You would rather choose some low-life girl than your own family!"

"A hundred times over," I said, groaning.

"All I have done, I have done for my children! For years I have protected you. Kept you alive. Sure my approaches were harsh but in order for you to survive you needed to be tough. I gave up *everything* for my kids."

I shook my head. "You made us fear you. You tormented us."

"Before you were born—when I was no Vampire and the world was simple—I was married to an abusive man, Anya's father. He nearly killed your sister and me multiple times. I would sit at the fire wishing for his death. Then one day a foreign man came into the little town. He was dark and mysterious, and I began to fall for him. He pursued me and after some time together he offered to turn us. I greedily accepted. I killed Anya's father that night. Gave up my humanity, became a monster, to protect my child."

"You became a monster for your own selfish purposes. You wanted power and the second you had it, you wouldn't let go."

"Hundreds of years have passed since I was turned, but men are all still the same. Your father wanted to kill you, Silas, did you know that dear? He called you a devil. He said anything that came from my womb had to die. The day after you were born, I found him standing over your crib, a knife in his hand. So, I did the only thing I could do to protect my child. I killed him, drained him of all his blood."

"You can't sway me. I know the tale, Anastasia told it to me when I was a child. You kidnapped my father off the streets and forced him to sire me. You tormented that man for years until he was able to give you a Dhampir child. Then once he had, you released him. My sister's only tale of your mercy."

"You will not believe me, no matter what I say? You will not join my side?"

"Never."

Mother sighed, her hand balling into a fist. "Then you leave me no choice."

Mother pulled out a large syringe from her pocket and injected its contents into my neck. Instant pain attacked my brain; my head felt like it was about to explode. I clutched my skull, fingers digging into flesh. I wanted it to end, but it just wouldn't stop. I screamed until my throat turned raw. I was losing control. Losing everything. Fading away. I was changing. My mind was no longer my own. And as Mother wished, I was metamorphosing into a monster. I had fought so long to keep my humanity but now it was gone. The scales had tipped, and I was a monster through and through.

CHAPTER 14

HARPER

I woke up to Silas' screams. They were raw and heartbreaking. I wanted in that moment, despite the pain and anger, to hug him, to tell him everything would be okay. I struggled against my binds.

I needed to help him.

Then it all just stopped.

Silas came to his feet, no longer clutching his head, and walked toward me. His eyes, my God his eyes. No longer were they beautiful jade pools; these eyes were soulless, devoid of color.

Completely white.

I stared at Silas as he mindlessly approached me. Gone away were his smiles and witty banter. This Silas was different.

"What did you do to him?" I shouted, afraid to hear the answer.

"Isn't it obvious, child," Lenora said. "I did the only thing I could to keep my son. I used the serum."

My heart stopped beating. "No."

"We are linked, him and I. For now and all eternity."

I shuddered. "Please God, no."

"He left me no choice," she said.

"You're a monster!"

"Lenora Ravnos." A male voice shouted, cutting our conversation short. "You are hereby sentenced to death on orders from the BPMI."

Without warning a bright light filled the room as flash grenades rained down. Lenora hissed like a wild animal and phased into a dark corner. BPMI Agents filed in the stadium, guns drawn and pointed at Silas and Lenora. A man with peppered hair parted the crowd. He was muscular and dressed in black tactical gear.

"Any last words, Lenora?" the man asked.

"Silas dear, show them your true form!" Lenora shouted from the shadows.

Silas screamed as the skin on his back began to move as if hands were pushing up under his skin. Large black bat-like wings exploded outward, flapping furiously. His nails became talons and his teeth razor sharp. His eyes didn't take on their red hue; they stayed soulless white. The BPMI agents took a few steps back as a dull hush fell over the crowd.

The crowd stared at Silas and, in the moment of confusion, he struck. Silas phased, throwing himself forward, tackling into a group of BPMI Agents. There were shouts and then the bullets flew.

I needed to free myself. I needed to help Silas. The drugs that Lenora had slipped me had finally cleared enough that I could focus to use my powers. I forced Heaven's Light into my palm and the rope binding me slowly began to burn.

A grunt filled the air as bullets struck Silas' thigh. Finally, the rope around my wrist gave way and I jumped to my feet. I leapt to the side, avoiding stray bullets.

Silas breathed heavily as blood flowed down his body. He extended his arms in front of him. Blood from the fallen agents around him began to move forward as if an invisible energy pooled it into his palms.

Silas was doing blood manipulation, a rare ability that only very few vampires possessed. His blood crystallized and he released them in a spray of red. Shards struck the BPMI Agents and many fell down, bleeding out.

"I can't believe I'm doing this," I said.

I charged forward grabbing a discarded gun and jumped on Silas' back. One of his milky white eyes took me in and he flapped his wings, lifting off the ground. I held on for dear life.

"Si, stop!" I shouted.

Silas gathered more blood into his palms and blasted a hole through the ceiling. Lenora, with a pair of her own wings, took to the sky and flew through the gaping hole.

"Good work son, we need the girl," Lenora said.

Silas grabbed my wrist, pulling me face-to-face with him. I stared into his white eyes.

"Silas please. I know you are in there."

Silas' eyes slammed shut and he growled. A moment later, his eyes sprang open, one of them now green.

Then something hit Silas hard from behind and his eyes turned milky white again. The jolt from whatever struck him was so strong his grip on my wrist loosened and I fell. I looked above me and saw a blaze of purple skirting around Silas. I closed my eyes, waiting for the ground to greet me. I hit something hard. I expected the pain to be unbearable, but I didn't feel anything at all. I opened my eyes. I was still alive. I was floating. Purple hair brushed against my face. Anastasia held me in her arms, bat wings protruding from her back.

She began to descend.

"Wait! We need to help Silas!" I shouted.

I looked to the sky. Silas had since gained control and was flying farther away.

"We fall back for now," Anastasia said.

"But—"

"I'm too weak to fight and so is Druze. We will need to regroup and go after him later."

"Then let me go, I'll go after him myself."

"You'd only get yourself killed," Anastasia said harshly.

"I don't care. We need to save him."

"We will, but you have to trust me."

Her feet touched the ground. I looked upwards as Silas became a small dot. Tears fell down my face. The BPMI Agent with the peppered hair approached us, a small battalion of agents behind him.

"Hands in the air where I can see them!" The BPMI Agent shouted.

I lifted my hands in defeat. Anastasia stood her ground.

"You will not harm us," she said matter-of-factly.

"Oh yeah," the Agent said. "And why not?"

"Because we need to become allies," Anastasia answered.

The Agent laughed, deep and hearty. "I would never align myself with a monster."

"Right now, you have a powerful Dhampir attacking Sable and a Vampire with syringes full of mind control serum. If she gets her hands on Sable's Alphas, life as we know it will cease to exist," Anastasia explained.

"Why would you care?" The Agent asked.

"Because Sable is my home and just like you I enjoy living. My Mother will stop at nothing to see that the whole human race is extinguished and every monster on the planet bows down to her," Anastasia answered.

The Agent's eyes squinted, anger flowing through him.

"I have an army waiting at my beck and call," Anastasia said. "If I simply give the word, they will kill you all. We have you outnumbered ten to one."

The Agent reached for his gun.

"Remember humans, we are stronger than you. Your men will die in vain, and Lenora will still be in control. Accept our alliance and we can stop her together."

Anastasia stuck out her hand. The Agent stared at it for a long moment before reaching out his hand and shaking hers.

"Caine. You can't be serious," one of the agents said in disbelief.

"You are to follow orders, not question mine," Caine barked. "For now we work alongside the Vampires to take out this new threat."

"Wait! You can't hurt Silas," I said, approaching Caine.

Caine stared down at me. "Who and what are you?"

"Her name is Harper. She is a Nephilim," Anastasia answered. "She will be our trump card at beating Lenora."

"How is this girl going to defeat her?"

"She is the key to Silas's heart. She can break the hold Lenora has over him. I saw it with my own eyes."

I nodded. "It was only for an instant but he returned to normal."

"Why does freeing Silas matter?" Caine questioned.

"Silas is her heavy hitter. Without him, Lenora will become sloppy, make mistakes. She cherishes him and losing him will be a major blow," Anastasia answered.

"Right. We stop the Dhampir, we weaken the Vampire. Men, regroup at HQ. Harper and the vamp will stick with me," Caine ordered.

Druze parted the crowd. Caine's men backed away, guns raised.

"He's with us," Anastasia said.

"And what the hell is that?" Caine said, gesturing to the one-armed seven-foot-tall man.

"A troll," Anastasia said.

Caine stared for a long moment. "Right, the troll comes with us too."

CHAPTER 15

SILAS/DARKNESS

I wanted to kill. To dismantle everything around me. To instill fear. I was Mother's little monster and I loved it. It felt so amazing to finally stop fighting. To finally be free. Silas and I were one and the same. I was Darkness, the vampiric side to him, and I was finally in control.

We landed in Bane territory, Mother at the lead. Wordlessly she commanded me to break down the door to Bane Manor and I did so with giddy joy. I launched a blood ball at the door, killing two guards instantly. *Oh, this is turning out to be a good day.* A small crowd of vampires and donors pooled in the foyer. Mother entered the room with a smile upon her lips.

"Where is your Alpha?" Mother demanded.

A woman with bright green hair parted the group. "Who wants to know?"

Mother snapped her fingers and with glee I pounced. I tore open the Vampire's neck, her blood on my talons.

Whispers filled the air.

"I am Lenora Ravnos and I am your new Alpha."

A laugh filled the foyer. A man with a scar over his eye and dressed in baggy clothes stepped out from the crowd. He approached Mother.

"You asked for their Alpha and here I am."

"Great," Mother purred. "Silas, get him."

***

Gabriel Bane's blood decorated my clothes. The Alpha was a boring fight, but I made Mother so proud. She stood among the weaker Vampires and they bowed at her feet in fear. She approached Gabriel and injected him with her serum. He screamed and his eyes became milky white. He rose to his feet, standing before Mother.

"Now that this is settled, you all have a very special mission. You will be storming the BPMI and taking them down once and for all." Mother turned to me. "*You* will bring the Nephilim girl to me."

I nodded my head, exiting the manor. I took to the sky. It wouldn't take long to locate Harper and once I did, she would be Mother's once more.

I returned to the planetarium and immediately caught her scent. I followed it like a hound, arriving at the BPMI Headquarters. *How interesting.* In the hour it had taken me to find Harper's scent, Mother's followers had already begun storming the HQ. I entered the front door, stepping over a dead agent. I was missing out on all the fun, but soon I would have Harper and would get to have all the fun I wanted.

I walked through the BPMI waiting area and entered a hall. I tracked Harper's scent until I came across a room. Her scent emanated from behind the door.

Let the fun begin.

I opened the door and stepped inside. Harper stood against the far wall. I flashed my fangs at her. She looked at me with sad tear-filled eyes.

"Harper," I growled.

The time I had been waiting for had finally come. *Harper will be mine.*

"Si, I know you're in there," she said, taking a step toward me.

I phased, charging her. Searing pain rippled across my back. I turned toward the source of the pain and found Anastasia, her sword at her side, dripping with blood, my blood. Anger tore through me. I launched at her and she phased. I matched her speed, bouncing around the room. I pivoted, setting my sights on Harper. Just as I was about to strike, another being phased in front of her.

Druze. He shielded Harper with his body, his back taking the blow. Druze hugged Harper, protecting her. I growled, slowing to a stop. Anastasia stopped as well, standing before Druze and Harper.

"Give it up, Silas. You're outnumbered," Anastasia said.

I released a roar. I closed my eyes, summoning blood to my hands. I created a large, crystallized spike and launched it at Anastasia. She stood her ground and slashed the spike with her sword, cutting it in half.

I smiled.

I opened my eyes, aiming the two spikes straight for Harper. She was as good as dead. The spikes flew through the air. Two loud pops sounded and my spikes burst into dust. Growling, I turned behind me finding a BPMI Agent. He aimed his gun at my head.

"Give up Silas," the Agent said.

I phased once more increasing my speed, this time aiming for Druze. I grabbed the troll by the neck and flung him at Anastasia. Druze landed on her in a heap, leaving Harper completely vulnerable. I slashed my talons at her.

My hand hit something hard, but nothing was there. I slashed again but couldn't hit her. I continued slashing at her.

"You like it Silas? It's my shield. The scientist here taught me how to create it," Harper said. "That isn't all I can do either."

Harper moved her hands in an arch. Suddenly, I felt pressure all around. She squeezed her hands close together and her shield around me grew smaller. I attacked her invisible box but it did no damage.

"Now!" Harper shouted.

A light breeze blew across my back. An opening. I turned around quickly only to find a feathered dart sinking into the skin of my shoulder. Instantly, I began to feel woozy and crashed to my knees. I reached out a taloned hand, a last attempt to kill Harper, but soon I was greeted by unconsciousness.

***

My eyes were finally able to open. My shirt was gone and my pants were in tatters, exposing my skin to the cold air of the AC. I didn't mind it though, it felt nice against my hot skin. I looked around and immediately felt enraged. I was in chains, hands above my head. My wings were tied behind my back, causing mild discomfort. I was in a new office. This one smaller than the previous. Chairs and desks barricaded the only exit. The walls were splattered with blood, but all the dead bodies had since been removed. The sound of foot-steps called out as a man with peppered hair approached me followed by that do-gooder girl, Harper.

I growled at them. Harper stopped in her tracks with a look of hurt on her face. *Good.* I continued growling. The man—his badge read 'Caine'—stopped about a foot away, just staring.

"Enjoyed your nap?" Caine asked.

I growled once more and began collecting blood into my hand. Harper created a shield around me. I thrashed about, but the chains held. I cursed her. *She will die. I will make sure of it.*

"Silas," Harper said, approaching me. She touched the edge of my prison.

"He's gone," I said, a smile gracing my lips.

"No. I know he's in there," she said, desperation in her eyes.

I would have to snuff that hope out.

"I am Darkness. There is no more Silas, he died the moment I was released," I said.

"Shut up! He's in there! I saw it with my own eyes!"

She created an opening in her shield and stepped into my prison.

"Harper don't," Caine warned.

Harper ignored him, closing off the shield before he could pull her out. Tears lined her eyes. I looked at her and laughed.

"Am I supposed to feel something?" I asked. "Boo-hoo, your feelings are hurt. Good."

I grinned, exposing my fangs. Harper's hands began to glow, and she touched a finger to my forehead. Instant pain wracked my body from her touch. I tried to pull away, but the chains held taught.

"Darkness," she said, staring me in the eyes. "As you probably noticed the only way to defeat you is light. And I have plenty of that."

Her hands began to grow brighter and more pain assaulted me. A harsh scream escaped my lips. Harper pulled her hand away and looked at me with hurt eyes.

"It's going to take more than some fancy light show to get me to leave. I could do this all day," I said, baring my fangs.

"Your choice, Darkness."

***

Harper spent the better part of an hour dousing me in her Heaven's Light. I passed out a few times but still managed to maintain control. I wasn't backing down, not without a fight. Harper was breathing heavily at this point, hands on her knees. Using Heaven's Light and keeping up a shield was obviously draining for her. If I could outlast her a little while longer...

Harper's shield dropped and she collapsed to her knees. This was going to be easy. Caine knelt down beside Harper, helping her stand. Harper balled her hands into fists, and I laughed at her frustration.

"You were so confident. How must it feel to fail?" I asked, grinning.

Harper punched my chest, hard, a ball of light exploding around her fist. I released another scream as my skin felt like it was being peeled away from my body. I took deep breaths, willing the pain away. I flashed my fangs, showing her she couldn't break me.

She took another step toward me and I braced myself for the pain, but it didn't come. Instead she pulled me into a hug, her face against my naked chest. Tears streamed down her cheeks. My heart began to race.

"I'm so sorry Silas," she said, "if only I had—"

"Harper—"

She looked up slowly, meeting my gaze. *No!* I could feel myself slipping. When I took over, I made sure to cast Silas out, lock him in a dark box where he wouldn't be freed.

"Silas?" Harper questioned, her eyes looking at me hopefully.

"He isn't coming back," I said, forcing Silas down.

"He's in there. I just heard him." She wiped the tears away. "I'm bringing him back."

Anger flooded my senses. In one swift motion I cut my wrist open, allowing blood to fall. A large shard of crystallized blood grew over my head, destroying the chains, freeing me. Harper gasped, taking a step backwards and in her moment of hesitation, I shot another shard into the ceiling, creating a hole. I shook the chains loose on my wings. In one swift movement I grabbed Harper and took to the sky.

It wasn't long before Anastasia joined us. She slashed at me with her sword and I dodged. While her back was toward me, I pivoted and raked my talons down her wings, cutting skin. With no wings left to fly on she plummeted to the earth.

Seeing her comrade injured, Harper fought against me, but I held on tight. I continued to where the air became thin. Her head began to droop as oxygen no longer reached her lungs.

"Si," she begged.

"He's dead."

Harper reached up a weak hand touching my forehead. "I command you to sleep, Darkness!"

A cold chill ran through my body. Sensing a moment of weakness, Silas broke free, regaining control. My eyes turned from white to jade green. A powerful wave of drowsiness washed over me.

***

We were falling, fast. I tried flapping my wings but all the energy was zapped from my body. Harper wrapped her arms around me and just as we were about to hit the concrete she threw up a shield, stopping the moment of impact. We touched down gently. I fought past the drowsiness to look around.

We were alone on a street about a mile away from the BPMI HQ. It was a residential area. The street was lined with trees and lamp posts to guide the way. Harper released her shield and I fell onto the asphalt. I couldn't run, couldn't walk, so I crawled. Guilt ate away at me. I had lied to Harper, kidnapped her, and to make it worse I had nearly gotten her killed.

I couldn't bear to look at her.

Harper's voice brought me to a stop. "Silas."

I didn't dare turn around. I could hear movement as Harper walked around me. She knelt down, facing me. Her face revealed nothing.

I wanted to scream. To ask for her forgiveness, but I had no right.

I turned away.

Harper's light, warm touch stopped me dead. Her hand held on to mine. She pulled it close to her heart and held it there. I could hear it beating loud, fast.

"Look at me," she said.

I turned to face her but couldn't meet her eyes.

"Silas, I said look at me."

I released a shaky breath, and my gaze locked onto her honey brown eyes. I stayed there, swallowed up by them. Harper threw her arms around me, pulling me into a tight embrace.

Her hug felt warm and inviting and in that moment all the pain and hurt melted away. Harper kissed me and my eyes slid shut to enjoy the moment. I never thought I'd live to feel this again. Her kiss was strong, passionate, and warmed my body. I held onto her, slipping my arm behind her back. My talons faded, transforming into nails. My wings cracked and began to slide back into my flesh. I kissed her around my fangs, careful not to cut her. Her sweet scent enveloped me, making me drunk. I didn't want this moment to end.

Harper pulled away seconds later, heat burning her cheeks. She looked around at the crowd of BPMI Agents starting to form. Anastasia soon joined them, limping and accompanied by Druze.

"Silas …" Harper began.

"I'm sorry," I whispered. "I nearly killed you. All things Darkness did, I can never forgive myself."

"We'll face them together, all the things you did. That wasn't you. You're back to normal now, even your eyes," she said, running her hand through my hair.

"Silas," she attempted to say again.

I raised my index finger to her lips, silencing her. "I love you."

Harper stared at me for a long second. "I love you too," she said, pulling me into another hug.

My heart fluttered and all I could manage was to choke out, "You do?"

"Yes," she giggled.

"But all the things I did …"

"They were pretty bad," she admitted, "but you came back for me." Harper smiled and my heart nearly exploded.

"I love you," I said again.

CHAPTER 16

SILAS/DARKNESS

With the BPMI HQ in shambles we were taken to a new temporary facility, a run-down factory located on the North Side of Sable. The factory was cleaned out, giving us no clue as to what it was once used for. The BPMI had quickly gone to work setting up shop, bringing in box after box of equipment. Anastasia's men were also calling the factory their temporary HQ, having used the tunnels to relocate.

I found myself in a small room, a large window behind me. Unlike in police stations I could see through the glass. A few of passing BPMI agents had stopped to gawk at me, though Caine quickly sent them on their way. I spent the rest of the day in Caine's company being interrogated.

"That's all I know," I said, leaning forward in the metal chair. "Why are you still questioning me? We need to stop her. At this point she's bound to have taken over every Alpha in Sable."

"I'm aware," Caine said, "but this type of situation requires that we have all the facts no matter how small so that we can shatter her plans."

I sighed leaning back in my seat.

"We will get her Si," Harper said upon entering the room. "Anastasia, Druze, us, and the rest of the BPMI will stop her."

Guilt ate away at me. Sable's BPMI was devastated after Mother's attack. Luckily, the BPMI Agents managed to gain control over the Vampires, but their numbers had dropped significantly.

The door to the office swung open again. Caine growled under his breath, "Damnit people, can I question in peace?"

"I found Mother's location," Anastasia said, entering the room. "My men are currently en route."

Caine nodded and shouted out the open door. "Wetzel!"

A woman, short and with blonde hair entered the doorway, shotgun in her hands. She nodded to Caine.

"Prepare the men to move out. Get the coordinates from the Vampire," Caine said.

"Of course, Sir," Wetzel said, looking over hesitantly at Anastasia. My sister smiled, flashing her fangs. Wetzel' s grip tightened on her gun.

"Don't worry little solider. I am not hungry now," Anastasia said, strolling out of the room, hips sashaying.

I rose from the chair and approached the door, but Caine blocked my path. "Not you. You stay here."

"What?" I said in disbelief. "You all need my help."

"No, we don't," Caine said. "My men don't feel safe working with a vamp as it is, but now you expect them to work with a Dhampir who was just under the enemy's control and could revert at any second?"

Harper stepped up behind me, grabbing my arm and squeezing it gently.

"Silas, he is right. It's too dangerous. Lenora could regain control again."

"I can't just sit aside while everyone risks their lives," I said.

"Look kid," Caine said, putting his hand on my other shoulder, "I know it's a lot to ask, but we can't risk it."

I sighed, walking over to a chair and taking a seat. As much as I hated to admit it, they were right. I was too dangerous and if I were under my mother's control again, I would only be a liability.

Caine approached me and set a Walkie Talkie on the table. "We're on channel four."

I nodded, not looking up. Harper sat down across from me.

"You aren't coming?" Caine asked. "We could really use a Nephilim's help."

Harper shook her head. "I need to keep an eye on Silas. Make sure he's good."

"Caine, we are ready for attack. The Vampire's men stand with us. Do we have your permission to advance?" The transceiver hissed.

Caine brought his Walkie Talkie to his face. "Copy that. My ETA is ten minutes. Begin advancement."

"Copy that sir. Starting advancement."

Caine turned toward us, nodded, then exited the room.

***

I couldn't keep my eyes off the clock. How long had it been? It felt like hours but in reality only thirty minutes had passed. I slammed my head onto the metal table for the fiftieth time that night.

Harper entered the room, two coffee cups in hand.

"Figured you'd need some coffee," she said, placing a cup in front of me.

I lifted my head from the table and nodded. I picked up the cup and took a sip. A searing pain attacked my tongue.

Harper frowned. "Should have warned you. It's hot."

I placed the cup down and gestured for her to do the same. She looked at me quizzically and I offered out my hands. She took them, her hands warming mine. A small smile graced her lips.

"Thank you for staying with me. Hell, thank you for saving me. I—"

"You don't have to thank me," she said, squeezing my hands lightly, "I'd do it a hundred times over if I had to."

"Darkness. He was so strong. I thought—I thought I'd be gone forever."

Harper knelt down in front of me. "Silas, you're strong too. You've resisted Darkness for so long."

I nodded and, unable to find the words, I rose from my seat, leaned over, and kissed her. Her lips were warm and she tasted of coffee. My heart beat loudly in my ears and her scent was dizzying. I pulled away quickly, my world spinning.

Harper smiled at me. "What was that for?"

"I almost lost you. I'm just glad to have you back."

She nodded lightly. "I'm glad that you are back Silas, but you must be exhausted. You need rest. I'll show you the makeshift sleeping quarters."

I grabbed the Walkie Talkie on the table, pocketed it, and followed Harper. She led me down a long hallway into an open area. Cots were spread out all over the floor. She led me to specific one off to the side.

"You can sleep in this one. I used it earlier."

I nodded, laying down. She grabbed a blanket on the end of the cot and threw it over me. In an instant, I was out.

✳✳✳

A beep.

I rolled on my cot, grumbling.

Beep.

What was that noise?

I tried to ignore it. My body was tired and aching. Being injured and nearly baked alive by Harper's Heaven's Light meant that I needed plenty of blood and sleep to heal. I took all I could get.

Beep.

I groaned, opening my eyes.

Beep.

I looked around, confused for a moment. I could've sworn the beep was close. Then it occurred to me: the Walkie Talkie. I glanced around me and found it face down on the floor. I lifted the transceiver and put it close to my ear.

A beep sounded followed by a broadcasted message:

"Come in Caine, do you read?"

"Caine has been captured. Lenora has forced us to abandon post in order to save his life," an agent reported.

"Damnit," another voice cursed.

"What are your orders Wetzel?"

"We stay back for now. Lenora is demanding to see the Dhampir," Wetzel answered.

"What of the Vampire lady and the troll?" Another agent questioned.

"They are busy holding off the Alphas," another voice said.

"Okay men, your orders are simple. Take out the minor monsters. I'll try to get in contact with the Dhampir. Keep a path clear and don't die," Wetzel said.

"Copy that."

"Dhampir," Wetzel said, "come in, do you read?"

I pushed the talk button. "I'm listening."

"Go to channel five."

I quickly went to the next channel.

"Dhampir?" Wetzel said.

"Speaking loud and clear," I said into the Walkie Talkie.

"I know Caine told you to stay put, but … we can't risk him. He is a valuable asset to the BPMI. You have to face Lenora and save Caine."

"Send me the coordinates and I'll be on my way."

"Silas?" Harper asked. I hadn't heard her come in, and I nearly jumped out of my skin.

"Harper … I—"

"You can't go out there—"

"I need to go, Harper. If my mother gets her way …"

Harper placed her hand against my cheek. "I know. Let's do this together. Stop her once and for all."

***

As promised Wetzel had cleared a path for us leading directly to Mother. As it turned out, Mother had made her base at an abandoned school. The majority of the monsters lay scattered on the ground alongside Anastasia's men and BPMI Agents. Wetzel led us to the main office. She stopped outside the door and turned toward Harper and me.

"Caine is inside. Do whatever you must to save him."

I nodded, glanced at Harper, and opened the door. I went inside the dimly lit office; Harper took my hand and I guided her through the rundown space. It wasn't a far walk, about ten feet, before we faced a large pair of double oak doors. An African Werewolf guarded the doors and stepped aside, allowing us to enter. I released Harper's hand and pushed the doors open.

Mother sat at a large wooden table. Caine was tied up in front of her, his back resting against the wood. A collection of bodies was strewn about on the floor. Cracked glass and debris coated the entire room. A flickering light swayed above Mother, part of its base pulled from the ceiling.

At our approach Mother looked up and smiled, revealing her blood-coated fangs. A chill went through my entire body. I stopped in my tracks. Harper wrapped her hand around my forearm, her warm touch bringing me back to life.

"Silas," Mother purred, "it's so good to see you. Are you thirsty? Take a drink."

I glared at her, remaining in place. Mother's smile faded and she turned her attention to Harper. Harper took a step forward, placing herself between me and my Mother.

"Hello Lenora," Harper said calmly.

"Nephilim. It is good to see you alive. I was worried I had lost my blood supply for the serum."

"Give it up Mother! It's all over. Your monsters are all nearly dead, and you are outnumbered," I said, trying to slow my quickly beating heart.

"Oh but Silas, I've been waiting for *you*. Our reunion is just what I need to win this war."

Mother's eyes turned milky white. An extreme pang of pain ran through my skull. I collapsed to my knees, clutching at my head.

Harper turned on her heels and knelt down to face me. She placed her hands on my shoulders. "Silas, you have to fight it. You're in control, not her."

I was fading fast. I could feel every part of me disappearing to be replaced with Darkness. I sucked in a deep breath a smile gracing my lips. "Guess who's back?"

✷✷✷

Harper released a choked breath and back peddled. "Darkness. Give Silas back."

"No can do, kid. Mother and I have plans. Starting off with capturing you."

I took a step toward her. Fear found its way onto her face. I felt giddy inside. Harper continued moving backwards until she was in a corner, nowhere left to run. Talons grew from my nails. I lifted my hand up ready to strike.

"Wait!" Harper shouted. "Aren't you tired of following Lenora's orders?"

I looked at her with questioning eyes.

"Think about it Darkness. She isn't as powerful as everyone thinks she is. She needs you or else she would have taken over by now. Dispose of Lenora and you can rule. Sounds an awful lot better than following orders," Harper said.

The little brat does have a point. I could rule all, be free from Mother's control. I could rule the world. Make people fear me. I can have anything I want.

Searing pain assaulted my eyes, fading from milky white to normal red. With Mother's control gone, Silas attempted to take over, but I pushed him down. It was my turn to play. I turned toward Mother and gave her my devilish grin. Mother frowned. Her eyes turned milky white once again. I began walking toward her.

"Your eyes. Red. How are they red? I control you!" Mother shouted.

"Not anymore," I said flashing my fangs.

"That's impossible. This serum is supposed to give me full control." Mother took a step backwards. "You obey *me*!"

I chuckled. "I bet you're wondering why this isn't working. You see, I am Darkness, I played your little game, but when there is something I want, I go for it. So far, our goals aligned, but now, I want it all. Money, women, power, everything—and quite frankly, you're standing in my way."

I phased at a speed even Mother couldn't match and grabbed her by the throat. I began to choke the life out of her. She clawed at my fingers, but I held on tightly. I'm not sure how long we did that dance, Mother struggling in my grip, me just laughing at her helplessness, but soon she began to go still.

"Darkness," Harper said, cautiously approaching.

I released a sigh. "I'm a little busy here."

"Stop. She can't hurt anyone like that."

"She can't hurt anyone dead either."

"Look, I know she hurt you and Silas, but this isn't right. Killing her would make you no better."

"I'm not looking to be better."

"Please, Darkness. You and Silas are one in the same, two sides to the same coin. You are his protector, and you know Silas should be at the wheel."

"Kid." I released Mother and she crumpled to the floor. She sucked in a large gulp of air but remained unmoving. I walked over to Harper, grabbing her by the wrist. "Silas has a real soft spot for you. It'd make me so happy to kill you, but I can already feel myself fading again. Silas is fighting hard to be free, damn bastard. He's really pissing me off, so I'll do this, as a symbol of my revenge."

I leaned in close and placed a kiss on her lips. She gasped in surprise and attempted to push me away. I savored the kiss for a moment but then I was gone.

***

I opened my eyes, finding a surprised Harper trying to push me away. I pulled away quickly, confusion running through me.

"Why am I kissing you? I mean, it was great, but why?"

Harper looked at me for a long second and released a small sigh. "Darkness is a dick."

She turned on her heels and approached Mother, still unconscious on the ground. She pulled out a needle from her back pocket, removing the cap. She inserted the shot into Mother's neck.

"Vervain," Harper stated. "That should keep her subdued for a while."

"So, we won?"

"Yeah. Darkness took out Lenora. Turns out the mind control serum didn't work on him. I think it was because you or him, well both of you, wow this is confusing. I think both you and Darkness were always more powerful than Lenora. You just needed the right incentive."

I reached into my pocket, retrieving the Walkie Talkie. "Come in Wetzel. It's over."

Seconds went by and soon we were surrounded by BPMI Agents. Wetzel began giving out commands and Mother was carried out the room, her body strapped down to a stretcher. Harper walked over to me, took my hand and led me out the room.

It was finally over.

EPILOGUE

SILAS

THREE DAYS LATER ...

I woke up feeling something I hadn't in a long while: happy. Harper lay beside me, her bare flesh wrapped up in a sheet. She was still asleep, her light breathing filling the air. I stared down at her, too afraid to move. This was peaceful, something else I never thought I'd be able to experience.

Caine's men had spent the better part of the last two days interrogating me and came to the conclusion that I wasn't going to go rogue again. With the work of the BPMI, a coverup had been performed, disguising the attack as major vandalism. Mother was detained and held in one of the BPMI Major Monster Holding Facilities. Her years of knowledge and secrets would be extracted and used to better assist the BPMI. Harper and I later returned to Ravnos Manor, where we spent the night together doing naughty things and purely enjoying each other's company. We were glad to be alive and treasured every moment of it, though the actions of Darkness still haunted me.

Harper's eyes fluttered open, drawing me back to the present. I pulled her into a light kiss and got up quickly, throwing some clothes on. Harper groaned lightly. She sat up and her sheet dropped, exposing her breast. I forced myself to look away and grabbed her a fresh set of clothes provided by Hema. Harper accepted them with a nod of thanks and quickly got dressed.

A knock sounded on the door minutes later. I opened it to find Hema herself.

"Was I disturbing something?" She glanced around the room, her gaze stopping on the bed.

I followed her eyes and saw our clothes strewn about from the morning's sexual escapade. Heat rose to my cheeks. Sensing my discomfort Hema looked down, staring at my feet.

"Your sister wishes to see you two. Follow me."

Harper and I glanced at each other but followed Hema down the hall. After minutes of walking we found ourselves in front of the late Lord Ravnos' room. Hema opened the door, placing her fist against her chest. Anastasia mimicked Hema. Hema excused herself and disappeared down the hall.

"Come in brother," Anastasia said, taking a seat at a desk.

I did as I was instructed, hand holding on to Harper.

"I'm glad to see you are feeling well," Anastasia said.

"Much better after all the blood."

"I called you to me to offer you a choice."

I looked at my sister quizzically.

"A choice?" Harper asked.

Anastasia nodded. "I'll cut to the chase. All the Ravnos owe you their thanks. You defeated Mother's tyranny and have freed us. We know we can never return to being humans but we can try to live like them, in peace. You can rest assured that the Beauregard clan's control serum research has been destroyed and the bounty over Harper's head has also been dismissed. As I'm sure you know Druze has disappeared. I lost track of him after the fight. And your friend, Fuzzy was it? He has been released from the BPMI Rehab Center. He sends his regards. Then that leaves you Silas. Of course, one option is that you stay here, help me rule, and regain peace in Sable. We could really use your help. You are the most human out of all of us. Or I will offer you the opportunity to leave, of your own accord. There will be no more house calls, no more disturbances. If that is what you wish, it shall be honored."

I stared at Anastasia for a moment in disbelief. "You mean that?"

"Yes," she answered.

I looked to Harper. She nodded, smiling.

"Thank you. As much as I want to put this whole experience behind me, you are right. Sable does need a reign of peace and we can bring that." I smiled. "But first, I think Harper and I need a little vacation."

Anastasia let out a breath. "Now, that that is settled, I will provide you with a car and some cash to help you two enjoy your time away. Now, please, leave and enjoy your time together. When you return we will begin a reformation of Sable."

I smiled at my sister, squeezed Harper's hand. We ran down the manor halls, smiles on our faces. We came to the front door. Hema was waiting for us there, a pair of keys and a credit card in her hands. She handed them both to me and I took them graciously. She smiled back and placed her fist over her heart.

"Best of luck to you," she said, moving back into the shadows, disappearing from view.

I threw open the door. The wind kissed my skin. I stood there for a moment, Harper beside me. I had been searching for my freedom for ten long years and now I finally had that, and more. We began walking down the steps to the car parked out front.

Harper and I got into the car and the engine turned over. She looked at me with happiness in her eyes.

"Where do we go now?" she asked.

"Anywhere we want," I said, pulling out onto the open road.

AUTHOR'S NOTE

Dear Readers,

I'm so glad you picked up my book! I hope you have just as much fun reading it as I had writing it! The idea for *Fanged: Blood and Water* came to me when the term "Fang Banger" randomly popped into my head. It was a curious phrase, and I knew I had to sink my teeth into it (pun intended). I ended up writing one scene where a girl, now known as Harper, asked for help from a Vampire after her clan was brutally murdered. Of course to the Vampire, now Silas, Fang Bangers were nothing but trouble, and he wanted nothing to do with the girl. Fang Bangers were simply blood banks to vamps and were known as a derogatory job. Though Silas looked down upon Harper, he soon gains sympathy for her. Over time the idea changed and expanded into the book you are reading now.

Before starting the book, I knew I wanted to write an urban fantasy. I loved the concept of monsters walking around in plain sight, and that humanity's ignorance was bliss. Well, at least, until they got eaten. Slowly over time, the book became an urban fantasy/paranormal romance novel.

There are three main themes throughout the book: Family, Love, and Humanity. I discovered these themes in my own life and knew I had to incorporate them into the novel.

Throughout the book, Silas struggles with the idea of family and love. I drew inspiration from my own life when I struggled with one family member who mercilessly bullied and harassed me. I grew distant and began to resent him. But over time, I healed, and now have a great relationship with all my family. I wanted to explore the idea of a found family, which is where the title kicks in.

The next theme, love, I also took from my personal life. I met my current partner when I was at my worst in 2016. I was suffering from trauma and didn't know how to cope. He helped pull me up from the darkness and into the light. I am so grateful to him, my family, and friends for all they have done.

My last theme of humanity was something I had to dig down deep to find. I always wondered when I was so young why people were always so mean, even when I had been so nice. In my years of learning and growth, I came across the word "humanity." Humanity is something that you earn, not something that is innately there just because you exist.

I knew I was the only person who could tell Silas and Harper's story, not only because I am the sole creator of them and their world, but also because I had experienced so much of what they had experienced. In the novel, Silas struggles with humanity. Silas believes being half-Vampire automatically makes him a monster, but he is wrong. Humans can be monsters too. They may not have fangs or blood-red eyes, but people give up their humanity every day for greed and lust. Humanity is something you have to work toward and build over time. We all have a monster we are battling, but what really matters is whether we give in. The hardest part for us, for humans, is knowing who is the monster and who isn't. Monsters are people who hurt others for their own benefit and take pleasure in it. It can be anyone: your neighbor, your teacher, or even you if you bow down to your inner monster.

When writing this book, I had to keep my target audience in mind. I knew this book was for adults, as I tend to write very dark storylines. It was also for anyone who wasn't queasy with gore, as people in the narrative tend to lose their heads quite literally. This is for fans of the subgenre urban fantasy. Lastly, and most importantly, this is for those who want diversity in their readings.

In the publishing industry, there isn't that much diversity. To be frank, it is a predominately straight, white space. I wanted to see people like me, especially bisexual women of color, for starters. I wanted to see different races, different skin tones, and different walks of life. This book is more than just an urban fantasy novel; this is a way of saying a diverse range of stories are meant to be shared by a diverse group of characters.

When writing this novel, I had to ask myself why my audience should read it. I wasn't sure at first. I want *Fanged: Blood and Water* to entertain, but that was the simple answer. Once I dug down, I realized I wanted this novel to teach people. Teach them that it is a choice of whether or not you become a monster. That it's okay to be different. That love doesn't have to be from your family. This book was meant to teach all the things I have learned.

I'm going to leave you with this last bit of advice. Know that in this crazy world, your family doesn't have to be blood. You can build a family around you with the people you meet. Your humanity isn't something you're born with, but rather something you earn over time by creating relationships and giving and finding love.

May you live a life full of magic!

Best,
Tianna Le'Ray

ACKNOWLEDGMENTS

I'd like to take a moment to acknowledge all those who took their time to support my book:

Miguel Garcia, Vanessa Sanjuan-Miranda, Cierra Collins, Cheryl Clarke, Zara Miller, Rahim Hython, Sandra Vasquez, John Ryan, Emily Baldys, Daniel Roberts, Karen Roberts, Christine Baldwin, Noemi Cruz, Suraaj Vyas, Joanne Bushell, Rosalind Maynard, Brittni Smith, Ian Blackman, Daniel Houston, Carrie Doll, Lena Gause, Sheree Tucker, Lisa Smith, Rayvaun Smith, Christina Cruz, Alfred Garcia, Brittney Steele, Phillip Layton, Stephen Roach, Aparna Bhanu, Alexandra Sherwood, Corey Landis, Denise Tucker, Kameke Tucker, Claudia Peters, Gwen Edwards, Rosland Ali, Susan Strickland, Wanda Williams, Rollanda Miller, Jean Eckford, Joann LeGall, Michelle Hahn, Gisel Garcia, Emily Kornblum, Jane Rasinki, Spring Meyer, Tendai Jordan, Jenny Blenman, Judith Phillips, Datheny Howard, Eslyn Downes, Elizabeth Blickenstaff, and Lesley Ivey

Another thanks to the anonymous donor who helped fund my book.

Thanks to all the hands that helped prepare *Fanged: Blood and Water*:

Jemiscoe Chambers-Black, Haley Newlin, Angela Mitchell, Kristy Carter, Sarah Lobrot, Stephen Howard, Kyra Ann Dawkins, Lelia Summers, Gjorgi Pejkovski, Rodel Farinas, Brian Bies, and Jana Jelovac

Special thanks to my Beta Readers:

Victor Neumann, Chris, and Cheryl Clarke

Lastly thanks to Eric Koester for his program at the Creator Institute, which was the guide to publish and create this book as well as New Degree Press for publishing my book.

www.ingramcontent.com/pod-product-compliance
Lightning Source LLC
Chambersburg PA
CBHW051453050726
47593CB00005B/2056